CONTENTS

The protagonists and the writers	iv
Overture	viii
Introduction	1
J. H. Oldham *by Andrew Morton*	3
John and Donald Baillie *by George Newlands*	17
Archie Craig by *Ian Mackenzie*	29
George Fielden MacLeod *by Ross Flockhart*	39
Robert Mackie *by Nansie Blackie*	53
Isobel Forrester *by Julie R. Baxter*	65
Lesslie Newbigin *by Duncan B. Forrester*	77
Ronnie Gregor Smith *by Davis McCaughey and Harry Wardlaw*	95
Maidie Hart *by Anne Hepburn*	103
Margaret and Ian Fraser *by Catherine Hepburn*	115
James Campbell Blackie *by Bill Shaw*	127
Mary Levison *by Robin Barbour*	139
Geoff Shaw *by John Harvey*	151
Editor's conclusion	165

The Protagonists

J. H. Oldham
ecumenist, diplomat, facilitator
extraordinary from 'Edinburgh
1910' to 1969

John and Donald Baillie
theologians in Edinburgh, St
Andrews and North America

Archie Craig
first General Secretary, BCC;
Chaplain, Glasgow University

George Fielden MacLeod
Church of Scotland minister;
founder of the Iona Community

Robert Mackie
SCM, WSCF, WCC leader;
ecumenical statesman

Isobel Forrester
lay reader and pioneer ecumenist

Lesslie Newbigin
Bishop, Church of South India;
missionary theologian

Ronnie Gregor Smith
theologian; editor, SCM Press;
Professor of Divinity, Glasgow

The Writers

Andrew Morton
Church of Scotland minister;
previously BCC, and Centre for
Theology and Public Issues, New
College, Edinburgh

George Newlands
Professor and Principal, Trinity
College, Glasgow

Ian Mackenzie
broadcaster and writer

Ross Flockhart
Church of Scotland minister;
sometime Director, SCVO

Nansie Blackie
previously SCM and lay staff
member, St Colm's College staff,
Edinburgh, and Central Committee
of CEC

Julie R. Baxter
lay woman and social-work teacher

Duncan B. Forrester
erstwhile Professor of Christian
Ethics and Practical Theology,
New College, Edinburgh

Davis McCaughey
SCM UK Study Secretary;
previously Professor of New
Testament and Master of Ormond
College, Melbourne
and **Harry Wardlaw**
previously Professor of Theology,
Uniting Church Theological Hall,
Melbourne

A TIME FOR TRUMPETS

Scottish church movers and shakers of the twentieth century

AN ANSWER TO A PREMATURE OBITUARY
FOR CHURCHES IN SCOTLAND

Introduced and edited by
NANSIE BLACKIE

SAINT ANDREW PRESS
EDINBURGH

First published in 2005 by
SAINT ANDREW PRESS
121 George Street
Edinburgh EH2 4YN

Copyright © the Contributors, 2005

ISBN 0 7152 0824 1

This book has been published with grant assistance from
the Drummond Trust, 3 Pitt Terrace, Stirling.

With support from the Russell Trust.

With support from the Baker Trust.

The right of the Contributors to be identified as authors of this work has been asserted in accordance with the Copyright, Designs and Patents Act 1988.

British Library Cataloguing in Publication Date
A catalogue record for this book is available from the British Library

Typesetting by Waverley Typesetters, Galashiels
Printed and bound by Bell & Bain Ltd, Glasgow

The Protagonists

Maidie Hart
lay pioneer in SCOW, WCC and
BCC

Margaret and Ian Fraser
Church of Scotland minister;
Christian basic communities world
expert; ecumenical pioneer and
writer; Margaret, his wife, was
his constant support in all these
activities

James Campbell Blackie
Edinburgh University Chaplain;
Professor of Christian Ethics and
Practical Theology, New College,
Edinburgh

Mary Levison
one of the first female Church of
Scotland ministers

Geoff Shaw
Church of Scotland minister;
Gorbals Group founder; First
Convener of Strathclyde Regional
Council

The Writers

Anne Hepburn
lay ecumenist and feminist

Catherine Hepburn
Church of Scotland minister

Bill Shaw
previously Professor of Divinity,
St Andrews

Robin Barbour
sometime Church of Scotland
Moderator and Professor of New
Testament, Christ's College,
Aberdeen

John Harvey
Church of Scotland minister;
erstwhile Leader of the Iona
Community

BCC	British Council of Churches
CCBI	Council of Churches in Britain and Ireland
CEC	Conference of European Churches
SCM	Student Christian Movement
SCOW	Scottish Convention of Women
SCVO	Scottish Council for Voluntary Organisations
WCC	World Council of Churches
WSCF	World Student Christian Federation

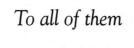

To all of them

OVERTURE

... for the twenty-first century, when the truth seems more appropriately communicated by poetry than by prose ... perhaps it always was.

> In this desert of language
>   we find ourselves in,
> with the sign-post with the word 'God'
>
>   worn away
>
>   and the distance ...?
>
> Pity the simpleton
>   with his mouth open crying:
>   How far is it to God?
>
> And the wiseacre says: Where you were,
> friend.
>   You know that smile
>
>   glossy
> as the machine that thinks it has outpaced
>   belief?
>   I am one of those
> who sees from the arms opened
>   to embrace the future
> the shadow of the Cross fall
>   on the smoothest of surfaces
>   causing me to stumble.

R. S. THOMAS

'Directions', from R. S. Thomas *Between Here and Now*, (Macmillan, 1981). Copyright © Kunjana Thomas, 2001.

INTRODUCTION

I have given this compendium the title *A Time for Trumpets* both to acknowledge and to celebrate our church visionaries of the twentieth century.

In a Scottish broadsheet newspaper at the turn of the twenty-first century, I chanced on a rare serious remark on church matters – normally the preserve of controversy or scandal. It claimed that the reformed tradition was and had been for decades ill-served in terms of vision and leadership. I strongly disagreed. Looking back, I began to hear voices and see faces, and it was suddenly clear how little we listened and how soon we forget.

Even in one life, lived not at all at the centre of things, I have known church people with such a profusion of gifts, clarity of vision, depth of commitment and springs of inspiration, that it seemed as if the journalist must have been living in another country. I discovered that very many agreed with my reaction. What about, people said, John Baillie or Archie Craig or Ronnie Gregor Smith or George MacLeod or ...? The list lengthened.

From this grew the idea to bring together under one cover a variety of reflections by a range of writers about some of these 'movers and shakers' of the last century. I've avoided the term church 'leader' as inappropriate within the reformed tradition. This itself is, of course, a source of some confusion to our secular press, which tends to transfer its obsession with a celebrity culture to church affairs, looking for bishops at least, but preferably cardinals.

Concern that as many of the writers as possible should have personal experience of those of whom they write, combined with the urgency of age, led me to abandon notions of even-handedness over theology, gender and denomination as principles of selection. In the end, the only principle is serendipity – in terms of my own experience. My motive behind the whole project is less piety towards our recent predecessors than profound conviction that their legacy to us is by no means merely of historical value but is highly relevant to the present and future of the church in the twenty-first century. Many of their ideas were not even tried; others were too briefly applied. Some – perhaps many – have resurfaced in recent reports accepted by the General Assembly of the Church of Scotland. It is informative, for example, to compare the war-time Baillie Report, the post-war 'Church Extension' movement, the thinking behind team ministries, the Gorbals Group, 'Tell Scotland' and the range of Aberdeen 1957 Kirk Week, with the content of the 2001 'Church without Walls' report. I cannot agree with the reactions of some of my own contemporaries: 'What's new? We were initiating these things fifty years ago.' True, but there is such a thing as 'a time that is come' – 'kairos'? At the very least, better knowledge of the tradition can but reinforce its strengths.

The writers between these covers know or knew their subjects to a greater or less degree – as did I. In one case, in Charlotte Brontë's words, 'Reader, I married him'.

So I made my choice – which could have included many more. I was heartened when the diverse and distinguished writers responded so readily. Their approaches to their subjects are similarly diverse and personal, and I did not regard it as my editorial function to tamper with this diversity.

NANSIE BLACKIE

J. H. OLDHAM

EDITOR'S PREAMBLE

'Ah, did you once see Shelley plain,
And did he stop and speak to you?'

My most memorable experience of a 'Shelley plain' was in the late 1940s when Davis McCaughey took me to lunch with Joe Oldham at the Athenaeum. Subsequently, I joined in discussions which Joe led at Swanwick Study Conferences. Andrew Morton, then a philosophy student, here surveys the sweep of Oldham's achievements during a working life of over seven decades.

At that time, I was most particularly aware of his radical reappraisal of the relationship between church and world embodied in the Moot and the Frontier Council. This seemed to me to apply some of the insights contained in Dietrich Bonhoeffer's letters, then recently published.

Andrew and I spoke at the Edinburgh launch of Keith Clements' definitive biography, *Faith on the Frontier*, in October 1999.

WHO?

It is sad that Scots who are well known around the world are often little known within Scotland. It may not be surprising, however, if for much of their life their talents are employed furth of Scotland. Joseph Houldsworth Oldham was one such.

What in the wide world is Joe Oldham's claim to fame? The quick answer is given on a sundial dedicated to him in the grounds of the Ecumenical Centre, the Geneva home of the World Council of Churches (WCC). It sums him up in three phrases – 'missionary statesman', 'foremost pioneer of the WCC' and 'friend of Africa'. Any one of these would be a resounding epitaph. Even those for whom his name resonates powerfully tend to know only one or possibly two but rarely all three of them; and there have been many who have known not any of these three but a fourth, which might be 'spiritual guide', for they have encountered him only as the compiler of the best-selling *A Devotional Diary*. But the sides of this many-sided man could be reckoned as even more than three or four, as this account of him hopes to show. For his was a richly productive life as well as a long one, spanning nearly a century – the ninety-five years from 1874 to 1969. I can do no more than trace its outline and hint at its significance for humanity.

FIRST YEARS

Joe Oldham was born in Bombay in 1874, the first of the five children of Colonel George Oldham and Lillah Houldsworth. His father retired early from India because of his wife's illness, and they settled in Crieff in 1884, when Joe was 10. After schooling at Edinburgh Academy, of which he was dux in 1892, he studied classics and philosophy for four years at Trinity College, Oxford. Early in his first year there, a visit by the American evangelist,

D. L. Moody, led him to commit himself 'definitely to Jesus Christ', and he became active in the Student Volunteer Missionary Union and the Oxford Intercollegiate Christian Union, of which he became secretary in his third year. On graduation in 1896, he was recruited to serve for a year as General Secretary of both the Student Volunteer Missionary Union and the Intervarsity Christian Union, working from London.

By now, his earlier career intention to return to his beloved India as a civil servant had been transformed by his dedication as a member of the Student Volunteer Missionary Union. He did return to India, but in a different capacity. In 1897, he was appointed by the Scottish YMCA to work in Lahore among students and government employees. He immersed himself totally in the Indian community – no, not quite totally, for after a year he was married there to Mary Fraser, whom he had met at Oxford and who was also a Scot with Indian antecedents, her father having been Governor of the Punjab and of Bengal. Joe's whole career might have been in India, but in 1900 after three years in Lahore both Mary and he contracted typhoid and were invalided back to Scotland.

1900s

He took this not as the end of his Christian missionary vocation but as an opportunity to explore that vocation more deeply by studying theology. As a member of the Free Church, which in that very year united with the United Presbyterian Church to form the United Free Church, he went to that church's New College in his own city of Edinburgh. Three years later, he graduated as Bachelor of Divinity with distinction, added a post-graduate year at Halle in Germany under the first-ever professor of the theology of mission, and then, like most newly qualified theological students, served for a year

5

as an assistant minister, partly in Dundee and partly in Edinburgh.

The United Free Church immediately recognised his special talents and appointed him in 1906 as full-time secretary of their highly innovative Mission Study Council, set up to encourage study of mission not just by students but by all its congregations. This church was in adventurous mood, not only because it was the product of a new union but also because it had shared the excitement of all the churches that had been involved in the missionary endeavours of the nineteenth century. They were now buoyed up by new hopes that the new century would bring a new world. Already the Student Volunteer Missionary Union had voiced the vision of 'the evangelisation of the world in this generation' and this aspiration was now gathering momentum.

An interdenominational missionary conference had been held in London in 1888 to mark the centenary of the missionary movement, and a larger one followed in New York in 1900 to usher in the new century. But now there were hopes of a conference that would be much more international and would take really binding decisions about world mission. A plan for this was put forward by a meeting of twenty Scottish missionary bodies convened by the United Free Church, and this was accepted around the world. It was decided to hold the event in Edinburgh, doubtless in part because the proposal came from Scotland, but also because, according to the record of the event, 'in the earlier missionary enterprise which evangelised Europe no country was more prominent than Scotland, and no country in proportion to its size has contributed so large a number of missionaries to the evangelisation of the world during the last century'. It was no surprise that the person appointed as full-time organiser of this event was the UF Church's Mission Study Council's secretary, Joe Oldham. Starting in 1908, he oversaw a two-year process of thorough fact-finding and analysis-making of all that was happening in the mission of the churches throughout the world, and he prepared and managed the event itself, which duly took place in 1910.

Much has been written about 'Edinburgh 1910', when 1,200 people from all over the world spent from 14th to 23rd June in the Assembly Hall on the Mound. History has confirmed that it was an epoch-making event. At the time, it had two major consequences – the intensification of worldwide Christian mission and the creation of worldwide Christian bodies and there is indeed currently a ten-year programme leading up to its centenary and reinterpreting its continuing significance. I pick out only one aspect of it. Its organisers, not least Joe Oldham, believed that, in the still young century, humanity had a choice between two ways of unifying the world. One was through the gospel the other was through the commercial culture of the West. They saw the need to work hard for the former, in face of the likelihood of the latter; their dream of the one was matched by their nightmare of the other, which would bring 'havoc that centuries are not able to repair'.

1910s

Whatever the effect of Edinburgh 1910 on the world, the effect on Joe Oldham was lifelong. Of course it could be said that, while it shaped him, he had significantly shaped it in the first place. At any rate, his subsequent career flowed from it. The conference immediately appointed him as secretary of the 'Edinburgh Continuation Committee'. In this capacity, in the following years he met with mission boards in the United Kingdom, throughout Europe and in North America. He also decided that there was a need for a major journal that would give living expression to 'the unity of the work of preaching the one gospel of the one God, who sent his only begotten Son to save the one human race and gather it into one holy fellowship'. And so in 1912 he created the *International Review of Mission*, a major quarterly that he edited from then on, and which still exists. It had substantial editorials from his pen, together with reviews and articles not only by missionaries but also by scientists and administrators. By this time, he was based in London and continued to be so.

The First World War of 1914–18 of course restricted his efforts and travels, but it also presented him with new challenges. Though he was not opposed to the war, he was concerned for the continuation of German involvement in world mission. So, when German missionaries were interned in India and expelled from Africa, he negotiated successfully with the heads of government of the allies for the non-confiscation of the German missionaries' property and for their return and freedom to continue in their former colonies after the war. In this, as in later negotiations with governments, he won so much respect from them that, though they were subject to his criticisms, they sought his advice.

1920s

In the next decade, this blend of criticism and advice and all his other gifts were given an even broader arena. For, in the course of 1920 and 1921, he and his closest colleagues succeeded in establishing an International Missionary Council as the permanent inheritor of the task of the 1910 conference, namely to enable churches throughout the world to act as one in their mission to the world. Again, the obvious choice of permanent secretary was Joe Oldham. His worldwide negotiations now took him farther afield – to China, back to India and to Africa, this last becoming now a powerful focus for his energies.

Already in 1916, in his first major book, *The World and the Gospel*, he had identified as an important issue 'whether the African races should create a characteristic life of their own or be made the tool of others'. Now he successfully organised academics, politicians, the press and the churches to oppose forced labour in Kenya. He then acted both as a mediator between the Europeans and the Indians there and as defender of the Africans, on the basis of what he called 'the paramountcy of rights of the native population'. He was even offered the post of Research Director to the Governor of Kenya, an offer which he declined. His African endeavours then broadened out. He encouraged the formation of an Advisory Committee on Native Education in Tropical Africa, which consisted of missionary representatives and colonial governors; he helped draft the 1925 white paper, *Educational Policy in British Tropical Africa*; he organised a conference of colonial administrators and missionary educators; and he created and became director of an International Institute of African Languages and Culture, which continued in being until just before the Second World War. When a commission was appointed on Closer Union Between the East African Territories, he was appointed to it and strongly influenced its final decision not to proceed with such a union, which would effectively have given power to the settlers at the expense of the native population. He also became involved in South Africa at the time of the Colour Bar Act, declaring that 'racialism is the deadliest enemy of a humane civilisation'.

In the midst of all this activity in the 1920s, he produced the two books which are probably his best known: in 1924, *Christianity and the Race Problem*, and in 1925, *A Devotional Diary*. While his African focus was strong, it was far from all-absorbing. As Secretary of the International Missionary Council, he was also maintaining a vigorous transatlantic or European–North American conversation on the future of the global mission. He summed up his view of this in 1929 in a document, *The New Christian Adventure*. Three messages ring out of it: (1) there is now a worldwide secular culture;

(2) the old distinction between the 'base' of mission and its 'field' (and between Christian and non-Christian lands) is obsolete, both base and field now being everywhere; and (3) the main agents of mission are laity. His critique of the dominant secular culture was that, in its human notion of mastery of nature, it neglected 'relationship'. In this, he was much influenced by certain European philosophers and theologians, of whom the best known is probably the Jewish philosopher, Martin Buber. This emphasis of his – on lively relationship with God, with one another and with the world – comes out in his later writings, especially in two books, *Real Life is Meeting*, published in 1941, and *Life is Commitment*, published in 1953.

1930s

In the 1930s there was a further broadening of Joe Oldham's energies, as the very positive movement to create a fully representative worldwide Christian body gathered momentum, and as at the same time the very negative movement towards totalitarianism and division in Europe increased its pace. The movement towards unity, which followed Edinburgh 1910, had three strands: one was the International Missionary Council, for which Oldham worked; the other two were 'Faith and Order' and 'Life and Work'. In 1934, the last of these, the United Christian Council for Life and Work, invited Oldham to chair a research committee to prepare a world conference on 'Church, Community and State'. The stark confrontation in Germany between a totalitarian state and the churches' gospel made this issue urgent. So, from 1934 until the conference took place in Oxford in 1937, Oldham devoted great energy to writing, enlisting other writing, speaking and organising, all in preparation for this conference, which had a long-lasting influence on subsequent Christian thought and practice about the state.

At the same time, he was engaged with others, notably William Temple, in planning to bring the different ecumenical strands together in what he had described as early as 1921 as 'something like a world league of churches' and which came to be called the World Council of Churches. He and his colleagues were working towards its inauguration in 1938, but in the event the threat and then reality of war postponed it until 1948.

1940s

One might well have expected that the onset of a Second World War in his lifetime would have dampened Joe Oldham's ardour, especially when one realises that by 1939 he was now 65; indeed he had recently retired from the secretaryship of the International Missionary Council. But in some ways the war stirred him into greater activity. Although it prevented international travel and negotiation and postponed the process of forming the World Council of Churches, it did not stop him from gathering people together within Britain. He had already started in 1937 to draw some of the most eminent thinkers of the day into conversation with one another; for the author of *Real Life is Meeting* was expert in encouraging and enabling people to meet, often those who otherwise wouldn't. So, he formed what he called 'the Moot' (an old word for meeting point). Its members included philosophers, theologians and church leaders, like the Church of England's William Temple and the Church of Scotland's John Baillie, together with the poet T. S. Eliot, the scientist Michael Polanyi, the sociologist Karl Mannheim and heads of universities, like Walter Moberly in Manchester and Hector Hetherington in Glasgow. This Moot continued to meet right through the war years until 1944, producing thought that had a great influence on post-war society.

A second initiative of his, which had an even broader influence, was his remarkable *Christian News-Letter*. Every fortnight for all six years of the war, he published this, with his own writing together with contributions from a wide range of the leading Christian thinkers of the time. It sought to give a Christian interpretation of the events of the day and to produce ideas so that 'a new society will be coming to birth even in the throes of war'. Very quickly, it gained 10,000 subscribers, who passed it on to others and often gathered in groups to discuss it.

Not content with this, in 1942, when the British Council of Churches was formed, he also formed the Christian Frontier Council, fearing that the British Council of Churches might become too dominated by clergy and solely concerned with internal church matters. The Christian Frontier Council was to complement this by bringing together lay people from all walks of life, Christian and non-Christian, so that they could face together the big issues of life and work. It too flourished, continued after the war and had a similar effect on the shape of post-war Britain.

LAST YEARS

His work was not yet over. The explosion of the first atom bomb in 1945 prompted the British Council of Churches to face up to the implications of this world-shattering event. Joe Oldham was asked to chair a group to prepare a report; and in 1946, at the age of 72, he presented the highly significant *The Era of Atomic Power*. Then, in 1950, now 76, he published *Work in Modern Society*, and in 1955, now 81, *New Hope in Africa* – for even in his eighties he was busy bringing young African specialists together with old ones in his own home. He and Mary, who were childless, had moved out of London to nearer the south coast in 1952 and eventually lived more quietly until her death in 1965 and his in 1969.

It is hard to imagine a more active and productive life. Wonder at it is increased when one discovers that for much of it he was severely deaf and dependent on a huge hearing aid. His importance was recognised in his lifetime by those who knew him and by his two old universities: Edinburgh gave him a DD in 1931, and Oxford in 1937. The *Dictionary of National Biography* included him almost immediately after his death.

CONVICTIONS

So, what was the significance of Oldham for humanity? Answers to this often highlight the word 'ecumenism' and point to the way in which the storyline of his life runs parallel to that of the modern ecumenical movement. This is not untrue, but it could be misleading if 'ecumenism' is understood, as often it is, as the ending of the damaging division of the Christian church. Of course that mattered to him, but for him it was part of something bigger. His ruling passion was, in the Student Volunteer Missionary Union phrase, 'the evangelisation of the world', which meant nothing less than the transformation of the world through the evangel. 'World' is a big word. For him it certainly meant the planet, as his planetary citizenship clearly showed (and incidentally that's what 'ecumenical' originally meant); but for him it implied not only planetary *out*reach but also philosophical, cultural, institutional and spiritual *down*reach. Evangelic transformation was intellectual *and* aesthetic *and* political *and* economic *and* psychological *and* anything else you can think of. The whole world needed to be changed.

But Oldham was equally clear that the church needed to be changed; so he was no less passionate about the evangelisation of the church. If he was sad about its division, as he was, he was no less sad about three other things – its ossification, its isolation from the world, and not least its clericalisation. Hence the energy he expended on galvanising lay activity and on crossing the church–world frontier. Indeed, he could be described as the great enemy of compartmentalisation. He held together things thought not to belong together. I pick out four.

COMBINATIONS

First, he combined a very personal evangelicalism, in the sense of an unqualified commitment of himself to Christ, with a rigorous and practical engagement with the great currents of contemporary culture and history, both in their philosophical roots and in their institutional expressions – all of which makes nonsense of the supposed antitheses *evangelical/liberal* and *evangelical/radical*.

The second combination was that he held together incredibly energetic, unremitting and wide-ranging activity with what today we call 'spirituality'. He was a 'man of affairs', if that word has not been spoiled, beavering away (a good word, for he was not an up-front, showy activist but a quiet and behind-the-scenes one), getting things done, almost a Mr Fixit. Yet the people who knew him only as the author of *A Devotional Diary* knew the real person.

His third combination was that of radicalism and pragmatism. Oldham's vision was radical enough, large enough. The early vision of the evangelisation of the world, to rescue it from its spiritual and moral vacuity, social irresponsibility and ecological insensitivity (all the things of which the world wars were a hideous revelation), and to change it into a profoundly Christian society – this was indeed a big vision. Similarly radical was his more particular vision of an Africa freed from racial domination and with its indigenous peoples empowered. But he married these revolutionary visions with painstaking report-writing, persistent coaxing of ministers and civil servants, and other similar ways of nudging policies forward almost inch by inch. He was, if you like, a gradualist radical, believing that real revolution is evolutionary.

The fourth combination was between such change-making action and theology. Thus, in the planning of the 1937 conference on Church, Community and State, in the Moot, in the *Christian News-Letter* and in the Christian Frontier Council, he brought the major academic theologians of the time together not just with church leaders but with politicians and educationists and business people – and indeed with one another! For him, theology and action belonged together.

QUESTIONS

Finally, I pose three live questions with which Oldham's life challenges me. First, when engaged in conflict and especially war, how do we oppose evil without aggravating it? In particular, how do we resist or combat the evil in the other side, while at the same time recognising the evil shared by all sides? In both the twentieth-century world wars, Oldham saw a greater balance of evil on the German side and resisted it, yet at the same time he saw the war as a consequence of a more widely diffused evil which included Britain, and so he took the war as a judgement and a spur to self-criticism and self-reconstruction. Do we have that double vision today?

Second, how do we overcome the clericalisation of the church? Oldham assumed that wisdom, including Christian theological understanding, was no preserve of ministers and priests but was widely diffused throughout the whole membership of the Christian community. So, he was much involved in seeking to garner this wisdom, bringing so-called 'lay' people together in a whole variety of gatherings of a face-to-face kind. What's more, he gave as much weight to such informal and unofficial meetings as to the church's formal, official and clerically dominated meetings. He applied this also to ecumenism, which began as a lay movement; so, when the churches formally accepted it, for example by creating the British Council of Churches in 1942 and the World Council of Churches in 1948, he was afraid that they would clericalise it. Although it was good to have the church leaders working together, there was a danger that they would not involve so broad a range of individual church people and indeed would squeeze out the visionaries and innovators and challengers. What is the balance sheet today, both in churches and in Churches Together, between the clerical and the lay, between the official and the unofficial, between maintenance and mission, and between meetings and meeting?

Third, why do some large gatherings of Christians not only change those who participate in them but also help to change the world? Oldham, who is famed for organising the great gatherings of Edinburgh 1910 and Oxford 1937, insisted that any such gathering should only be held under two conditions. These were – that it be informed by thorough research that preceded it, and that it include decisions on two or three strategic actions that would follow it. It was these two disciplines, rigorous preparatory thinking and tightly prioritised decision-making, that made these events so effective and such good value for money. Are today's church and ecumenical assemblies similarly research-informed and action-focused, as well as relationship-deepening?

SO?

I have always been sceptical about the 'great men' (and I do mean 'men') approach to history; but the life of Joseph Houldsworth Oldham persuades me that some individual people can have a pivotal role in historic social change.

ANDREW MORTON

JOHN AND
DONALD BAILLIE

EDITOR'S PREAMBLE

John and Donald Baillie were presiding figures in the immediate post-war church life of Scotland. I met John in several contexts; a slight but commanding figure, he was recognised well beyond his own country as the best kind of church statesman – wise, humane and deeply spiritual. His books on my shelves are among the most worn. As the fiancé of one of his students, James Blackie, I used to be invited to the enjoyable evening parties given by him and his wife, Jewel, at which we played intellectual games, feeling somewhat inadequate. These occasions were not, however, nearly as intimidating as those hosted at similar functions a few years later in New York by Paul Tillich.

Donald's gentle presence spread, like his theological ideas, far beyond St Andrews. I remember well his contributions to the Dollarbeg conferences initiated by Isobel Forrester.

Both brothers gave a notably temperate and ecumenical character to Church of Scotland attitudes during this period. George Newlands here reminds us of the essentials of their theological thought and emphasises its continuing relevance. His volume, *John and Donald Baillie: A Transatlantic Theology*, published in 2002, is invaluable as a quarry of information for those who did not know them and full of fascinating reminders and fresh perspectives for those who did.

John and Donald Baillie were among the most significant Scottish theologians of the twentieth century, and indeed since John Mcleod Campbell. They were outstanding among a series of distinguished scholars – John McIntyre and Tom Torrance, Donald Mackinnon and John Macquarrie, Ronald Gregor Smith and the magnificent Hugh Ross Mackintosh. I want to suggest here that in the Baillies the Scottish theological tradition reached a peak and a maturity which it urgently needs to recover if it is to provide any effective input into the theology of the next century beyond the familiar replaying of an all too parochial tune. In the tradition of the Baillies, I shall claim, there are resources to overcome the impenetrable fog of sub-Hauerwasian post-liberalism which sometimes appears to be about to engulf British systematic theology at the beginning of the millennium.

John and Donald Baillie were born in the Free Church of Scotland manse of Gairloch in 1886 and 1888 respectively. Though John later recalled 'a rigorously Calvinistic up-bringing', mainly by their mother who was very soon widowed, there were also astonishingly liberal strands in nineteenth-century Free Church culture and a huge respect for learning, which drove the brothers through brilliant academic careers in school at Inverness and university at Edinburgh, both graduating with Firsts in Philosophy, with distinction in Divinity and winning every possible prize, medal and fellowship in sight. They both became assistants in the Philosophy Department, and spent some time in the YMCA in France during the First World War. Both wrote copious poetry and delighted in literary circles of the sort that were pretty standard in the pre-war period.

There the path diverges. John married in 1919 and immediately went off to Auburn Theological Seminary in New York State, being ordained in the Presbyterian Church there in 1920. There followed six years of intensive

JOHN AND DONALD BAILLIE

teaching and research in theology, culminating in *The Roots
of Religion in the Human Soul*, and a large-scale work on
The Interpretation of Religion, completed in 1925 but not
published until 1929.

These books reflect an extraordinarily wide cultural
and theological experience encompassing the Calvinist
manse, the strikingly liberal tradition of Arts and Divinity
in Edinburgh before the war, the impact of four years with
the YMCA in France, immersion in American culture – its
poetry and politics, the polarisation of church politics in the
Fundamentalist debate, and participation in conferences
on the social gospel in New York in the early 1920s, long
before such issues came to centre stage in church circles
elsewhere.

John moved to Toronto in 1927, partly perhaps to be
near the support of old friends from Scotland (his wife
was in a sanatorium with TB from 1923–30, and looking
after their only son was not an easy task), partly too
because of the challenge of a new ecumenical college in
the newly United Church of Canada. Gospel and culture,
social issues and ecumenical concern were to be the focal
points of much of his later work. Return to America to the
Roosevelt Chair at Union Theological Seminary in New
York, at that time arguably 'the world's greatest theological
seminary', provided a forum for theology from which, along
with Henry Sloane Coffin, Reinhold Niebuhr and Pit Van
Dusen, he was to have a major impact on Western theology
for the next two decades.

In fact, John returned to Edinburgh in 1934. But the
transatlantic links remained very strong, and through
visits and letters the four exerted huge influence on the
new World Council of Churches, along with their friend
Bishop Henry Sherrill and others. Baillie, Coffin, Niebuhr
and Van Dusen differed in emphasis in several ways. But
they agreed on a *via media* between extreme liberalism on
the one hand, which they regarded as a dilution of the

19

gospel, and a narrow Barthianism on the other, which they regarded as an over-reaction to an over-reaction.

The overarching theme of the presence of God to faith was central to John Baillie's next three books, *And the Life Everlasting* (1933), *Our Knowledge of God* (1939) and *Invitation to Pilgrimage* (1942), while the emphasis on spirituality was manifested in *A Diary of Private Prayer*, which sold tens of thousands of copies, (and is still in print) a devotional work combining honest self-examination with concentration on God's reconciling grace.

The next step, centred on John's Moderatorial year of 1943, was the report of the Baillie Commission on *God's Will for Church and Nation*, which combined critique of the Nazis with a programme for social reconstruction after the war, a programme echoed in the Beveridge Reports. The Report recognised the difficulty in applying Christian principles in society, and took the route of 'middle axioms', which should 'exhibit the relevance of the ruling principles to the particular field of action in which guidance is needed'. An example is that 'Economic power must be made objectively responsible to the community as a whole'. The result is 'the clear declaration that the common interest demands a far greater measure of public control of capital resources and means of production than our tradition has in the past envisaged' (page 157, from 1944).

The subject matter of the Report echoed visits to Germany in the 1930s and conversations with both sides in the German Church struggle, numerous Church of England and ecumenical gatherings – not to mention the Moot, an influential forum which met in Oxford in the late 1930s and early 1940s. Members of the Moot regularly included J. H. Oldham, its founder, John Baillie, Eric Fenn, H. A. Hodges, Karl Mannheim, Walter Moberly and Alec Vidler, but there were others, including T. S. Eliot, H. H. Farmer, Donald Mackinnon and John Middleton Murry.

Against this formidable public international career in theology and church, it may seem that the work of Donald Baillie is a pale shadow. Donald suffered from poor health all his life and was shy, modest to a fault and always self-deprecating. Yet his books demonstrated a keenness of intellect and imaginative capacity which some have thought better than anything in John's writings; and his letters to his brother, always a great source of counsel, reveal a penetrating and often devastating capacity to sum up people and situations in the sharpest possible focus.

After being invalided out of the YMCA in France in 1917, Donald became a parish minister in Bervie in Kincardineshire in 1919, moving to Cupar in Fife in 1923, Kilmacolm in Renfrewshire in 1930 and then to a Chair of Systematic Theology at St Mary's College, St Andrews, in 1934, where he remained until his death in 1954.

Like John, Donald had spent semesters as a student in Germany, in his case in Marburg and Heidelberg; and his fluency in German led to contributions to the translation of Schleiermacher's *The Christian Faith*. *Faith in God*, a study of the anatomy of faith, published in 1929, established Donald as a serious contributor to systematic theology. Apart from some articles and works for church publications the only other major book published in his lifetime was *God Was in Christ* (1948), a book at once hailed for its clarity and elegance of exposition of the central issues of Christology, and one of a few British theological books translated into German, in 1954. However, the posthumous *Theology of the Sacraments*, together with two volumes of simple but profound sermons, *To Whom shall We Go?* and *Out of Nazareth*, served to confirm Donald's reputation as a major theologian. In addition, he edited the *Intercommunion* Volume of the WCC Commission on the subject which he chaired (1954) and produced a splendidly evocative *Memoir* of David S. Cairns.

It may be said that while John was at his best on the larger public stage, as theological lecturer or church politician, Donald was most effective in small groups, where his humour and the warmth of his personality inspired generations of students, notably at SCM gatherings, in which he was constantly involved from the early 1930s onwards.

The Baillie brothers were very close throughout their lives, and very sympathetic critics of each other's work. They shared a common theological outlook, often characterised, quite accurately, as liberal evangelicalism. Though John's writing more often dealt with matters of method and Donald's with substance, both were concerned to maintain a proper balance between faith and culture, the gospel and society, in which extremes of liberalism or conservatism were avoided. They were sensitive to theology in context, and could deploy arguments from the Barthian theology which came to have such an influence from the early 1930s, when this seemed right. But both deplored any sort of exclusive or dogmatic narrowness, either from fundamentalism or from liberal illusions of finality.

There is room here for only a brief selection from the Baillies' writings. I choose for illustration one text only from each. When we turn to John Baillie's last book, the Gifford Lectures published as *The Sense of the Presence of God*, we find a characteristic combination of an appeal to experience with an exploration of rational grounds for belief in God. A brief synopsis should perhaps indicate the flavour of the argument. Chapter 1, '*Knowledge and Certitude*,' deals with some of the most basic problems in the philosophy of religion. Knowledge seems to imply certitude but often does not go beyond probabilities. The concept of faith always contains both the idea of knowing and the idea of not knowing fully. 'No Christian, then, can say that he knows nothing' (p. 5). But equally, 'all human thinking is defectible' (p. 6). There are indeed certainties, in the natural sciences, in moral and especially in our religious convictions. A distinction is drawn between knowledge of truth and knowledge of reality. Our knowledge of the realities is primary, and our knowledge of truths concerning them secondary.

But does it work? Turn to Chapter 2, 'The Really Real'. Many have doubted our knowledge of any reality, certainly any beyond what can be verified by the methods of natural science. But what about the conviction that honesty and loyalty are required of us all? Moral convictions are central. Here, reality presents itself to us, requiring concern for others. This phenomenon is described further in a chapter on 'The Range of Our Experience'.

Early man felt himself to be at one with nature, not alien from it. 'Our total experience of reality presents itself to us as a single experience' (p. 50). Analysis of individual elements comes later. This is especially true of moral convictions. The point of this train of argument becomes clear by the time we reach Chapter 4, 'The Epistemological Status of Faith'. How do we 'reason things out?' Procedures for verification and falsification are discussed. 'A faith that is consistent with everything possible is not a faith in anything actual' (p. 71). Complete agnosticism is less frequent than we often imagine. For Baillie, the ultimate refutation of doubts is theological and incarnational. The claim made upon me by the presence of my neighbour is made by unconditioned being, by God. It now becomes possible to consider 'The Nature and Office of Theological Statements' (Chapter 5). Faith is 'an awareness of the divine presence itself, however hidden behind the veils of sense'. God reveals himself within a tradition and a community. The indirectness of faith's apprehension of God is explored through the Bible, Aquinas and Kant. Hegel and others in the nineteenth century are now invoked, and then in the twentieth. The result is a characterisation of theological language as analogical or symbolic.

Chapter 6 is then entitled 'Analogy and Symbol'. 'In the widest sense of the term all language may be said to be symbolic' (p. 113). But not all theological statements are analogical. Despite being known in, with and under other realities, yet there is a certain directness in apprehension of God. However, this two-way communication is in the nature of the case internal to the mind of the believer, and is always open to doubt on the part of the non-believer.

Chapter 7, 'The Framework of Reference', seeks to relate theory to practice. Christianity is a way of living. Love of God is always related to love of neighbour, and beyond this to a new humanity. This leads on to 'meaning and reference'. The gospel needs to be translated into the language of the present. Otherwise it is inevitably dismissed as irrelevant to contemporary life. In particular, it is important not to confuse dogmas with the primary perceptions of faith. Chapter 9 raises the wider issue of 'Faith and the Faiths'. The Greeks and the Romans developed philosophies of religion. Did they have a true knowledge of God? What does it mean to speak of Salvation in a name? (Chapter 10). For Baillie, there is some awareness of God in 'the pagan religions', but the Way of Christ is decisive. 'It is Christ himself that has created the world's desire for him' (p. 209).

Chapter 11 deals with Providence. Scientific and religious accounts of the world complement one another. Through modern physics, 'contradiction has been turned into complementarity'. What others may see as coincidence, Christians will read as providential. This naturally brings Baillie to a chapter (12) on Grace and Gratitude. 'He lov'd us from the first of time, He loves us to the last.'

'Gratitude is not only the dominant note of Christian piety but equally the dominant motive of Christian action in the world' (p. 236). This is *imitatio Christi*. We should also recognise vestigial forms of gratitude in those who are not explicitly Christian. The last chapter, 'Retrospect', reconsiders the argument. Analysis and clarity in linguistic analysis. But neither is Barthian exclusivism. Faith is trust. Propositions are necessary but not sufficient. We have to do with 'a God whose living and active presence among us can be perceived by faith in a large variety of human contexts and situations'. Baillie ends characteristically with Vaughan's prayer, 'Abide with us, O most blessed and merciful saviour, for it is towards evening and the day is far spent . . .'.

Donald Baillie's *God Was in Christ* (which echoes in many respects John's *Jesus Christ in Modern Christianity* of 1929) stands with John McLeod Campbell's *The Nature of the Atonement* and H. R. Mackintosh's *The Person of Jesus Christ* as representing the best of Scottish Christology in the modern era. Baillie was concerned to stress that God was really, concretely involved in all the risks and uncertainties of particular occasions in human history. This led him to emphasise the individual and complete humanity of Jesus, despite the theoretical advantages offered by concepts of impersonal humanity. He focuses on the fatherhood and the Love of God, and on Jesus' spiritual struggle as involving the conflict between the divine love and evil. He underlined the paradox of grace, the relation of the cross to the life of Jesus, and the balance of subjective and objective in atonement. John Macquarrie, in the same succession, summed it up in this way: 'It is not surprising that this book of Baillie's has attained to the status of a modern classic, for it combines the post-Enlightenment approach to Christology "from below" with a deep spiritual sensitivity' (*Jesus Christ in Modern Thought*, p. 329).

After the Baillies' deaths, systematic theology in Scotland came increasingly into the hands of a neo-Barthian school. More recently, the post-liberal writings of Alasdair MacIntyre and Hauerwas on the one hand, and the philosophical programmes of the so-called 'reformed epistemologists' and their supporters on the other, have proved attractive to a church and a theology which felt an urgent need for retrenchment in the face of plummeting church attendance and the perils of pluralism. Ecumenical progress was hindered, partly by association with triumphalist theology. With some honourable exceptions, the centre moved sharply to the right.

What, if anything, may be learned from the Baillies for the future? Both John and Donald were concerned to do theology in context, and to look to the future. They would not be interested in a repristination of their own detailed arguments, which were fashioned for their time. Indeed, John notes already by 1939 that references to the debates of the 1920s have gone from his work, since the students of today face new challenges. Yet there remain basic decisions about balance to be made, which have important similarities in different generations. Is theology to be exclusive, standing firm in one of Alasdair MacIntyre's Benedictine oases, *contra mundum*? Is theology to be deployed in the restoration of a Christendom which is long gone, and which proved also to have disturbingly totalitarian implications? John and Donald Baillie would, I think, be suspicious of each of these options.

Their work would appear to me to point to a theology and a church which remains both resolutely liberal and resolutely evangelical. This would mean resistance to an easy assimilation with the prevailing culture, in the name of the vulnerable Christ who is the judge of all exploitation and domination which is so common both in state and in church. This would also mean resistance to a complacent retreat to the calm paradise of the blessed, in a church and theological framework in which all answers are known in advance, and all nonconformists are excluded.

In the face of pluralism and fragmentation in the modern world, there is an attraction in various forms of totalitarianism. We have already seen at least two forms of this in the twentieth century. John Baillie insisted that we should not attempt to respond to these movements with a form of Christian totalitarianism. Donald was, if anything, even more insistent. There may be a promising path for the future in the direction of what can be programmatically described as a liberal engaged agonistic Christological multiculturalism. This is the direction which is suggested to me by the Baillies and by their friends Niebuhr, Coffin and Van Dusen. It is a stream of theology which, in my view, needs to be heard in theology and church today.

GEORGE NEWLANDS

ARCHIE CRAIG

EDITOR'S PREAMBLE

I was introduced to Archie Craig, an indisputable member of my pantheon of the great and the good, by Ian Fraser when I joined the Scottish SCM staff in 1947. Archie Craig was starting his decade as Lecturer in Biblical Studies at Glasgow University, where he had already become widely known as Scotland's first full-time University Chaplain from 1929 to 1939. In the First World War, he had gained both an MC and pacifist convictions, then subsequently ministered in two parishes. Of strong ecumenical conviction, he worked in London from 1939 to 1946, first as General Secretary to the Church's Commission on International Friendship and Social Responsibility, then to the new British Council of Churches. He returned to Glasgow as deputy Leader of the Iona Community, where his remarkable pastoral gifts complemented the more extrovert characteristics of George MacLeod. As Church of Scotland Moderator in 1961, he made official visits to Pope John XIII – (two of a kind?) – and to the oriental Patriarchs in Jerusalem.

Others have written about Archie Craig, principally Elisabeth Templeton in *God's February* (BCC/CCBI), but in this vivid picture of him in his nineties Ian Mackenzie brings to life the qualities that made him an exemplar of Christian leadership for his own time and the twenty-first century as well.

A QUESTION OF BALANCE

Archie Craig didn't quite make it to the top. He was, of course, Moderator for twelve months, but even in that role he seemed content to moderate, unaware apparently that there was a gallery to play to. He had, it is true, a ground-breaking meeting with the Pope; but, being ecumenical by nature, he made it seem like the kind of natural encounter you might have any day on the top deck of a Glasgow bus. He may have known everybody who was anybody, but did he succeed himself in becoming famous for being famous? His intellect didn't lead him to a professor's chair; in the university world, he laboured modestly at lecturing and exercising pastoral care. He was masterly in inter-church discourse; but, though I can see him as a fine Cabinet Secretary, diplomacy does not lay down a carpet to renown.

But his capacity for magisterial speech? His precision of wit elicited from audiences smiles of recognition of a disclosure rather than belly-laughs. He would have regarded manipulating a crowd into jocosity with the same distaste as manipulating it into belief. At the root of these failures to exploit promising situations, there lurked a seminal deficiency: the absence of a power drive, or, as I can imagine him revising that judgement, the presence of its effective submission to Grace.

Even in the pulpit, he wasn't assaulting your soul, he was having a conversation with your intelligence. When praying, he wasn't dictating an agenda, he was having a conversation with the Almighty, one the latter would find more interesting than most. It wasn't that this civilised man was incapable of enhanced language, even rhetoric; but it emerged from thought. There was emotion, but it was not to be set loose on other people until it had been taught manners in his mind. As a speaker about profound things, he was a connoisseur's connoisseur. Yet, because he was a clear thinker, his ideas were as accessible to nobodies as a tumbling Highland burn on open moorland; ironies, paradoxes, arguments, simplicities, shadows and light sparkled and glinted in one transparent flow; and his jokes were delectable. He walked humbly with his God, his brain and us.

That, at least, is the profile of him I built up over the years, hearing him at SCM conferences, at General Assemblies and in the pulpit. In all these situations, what gave special pleasure was his turning the ignition key in the brains of his listeners by ingesting an argument through his ears, chewing it through his intellect and ejecting it with turbo-charged refinements through his moustache. Despite his best efforts to avoid charisma, he invariably failed to achieve dullness. All this was apparent to me without meeting the man. Then suddenly I got to know him well. For two days. When he was in his nineties.

Before the end of my sixteen-year stint running the BBC's religious output in Scotland, I was encouraged to make a series of twenty-six films called the Quest. Archie was the first victim we visited to discuss the project, and subsequently he was the first we filmed. I put him first for three reasons. First, since I had an inkling of his penetrating perception, I craved – I don't think that's too strong a word – an honest answer from him to a question that was waking me up in the small hours: was the whole concept of such a huge film enterprise about God a notion of such pretension as to doom it to pomposity or, worse, ambiguous waffle? If Archie Craig gave it his imprimatur, we would go for it. Second, there was his great age; I would never forgive myself if illness or death pipped us to the post. But, third, I was clear that Craig had 'class'. There might be diamonds to mine.

The producer and I turned up at his Doune home for the recce. I was nervous. Being nervous wasn't my thing. My job required me to meet the world and its wife. But

I was in some awe of this towering figure I was now to face for the first time. When he opened the door, what I saw was a sort of stooping theological Cary Grant, crossed with a Border collie. Immediately we clicked. It either happens or it doesn't; but the range of his friendly antennae encompassed, I sensed, an unusually wide swathe of the human race. There wouldn't be many he didn't click with.

He arranged us in a beautiful sun lounge facing the garden. It was bathed in light; and so, I observed, were his face and, more unexpectedly, his voice. What really took me aback, however, was the realisation that he was amused. People, be they ever so eminent, are normally tense or at least wary when confronted by a broadcaster who may be about to expose them. If they are experienced, they cover it up with bonhomie or business-like bustling. If elderly, they fuss about unimportant details. Here was this guy in his nineties, fussed about nothing, regarding me with an amused detachment, and apparently waiting for something interesting to happen. But the interesting move was his. 'I'm honoured', he said, 'that you've come out of your Tower of Trebizond to visit me in deepest Doune.' Ignoring the first half of the remark, I asked: 'You're surprised that I want to seek out a guru of the age?' The eyebrows twitched: 'And which age was that? No, don't answer. In any age, I was never one of your most visible churchmen.' 'Your visit to the Pope was visible.' 'Now, Mr Mackenzie, don't disappoint me by telling me you want to talk about that.' 'No.' 'Good, because one of the reasons I'm intrigued by your Quest is your own comparative invisibility compared to your predecessors in the religious broadcasting world; they were not so backward at coming forward. Yes, I know about these things. Being a museum piece, I am regarded as a safe pair of ears to be told what goes on, and I gather 121 and those of that ilk regard you as an enigma because you do not reveal an obsessive interest in church politics.

Well, that's my inclination too; if Jesus was a politician, he wasn't a very successful one.'

And he was away, into theology, via that startlingly *ad hominem* opening. To say I was engaged is to put it mildly. After an hour's conversation in which he blessed the Quest because he'd had a lifelong belief that dialogue was the highest form of communication, he said: 'Tea, I think', and turned to engage with my lady producer. 'My wife is not entirely with us these days. Would you be so kind as to go to the kitchen while I fetch her, and would you help her to make the tea, and then serve it, in such a way that she has the dignity and pleasure of thinking she is totally in charge?' In due course, the producer being a natural in this situation, the tea ceremonials were conducted with tender loving care; and, logistics for filming agreed, we parted. I felt I had been hit to the boundary by a velvet fist.

That was the first of the two days I got to know Archie Craig. The second was some months later when, all recces completed, we turned up to film at Doune. Archie was calmer than a 1960s hippie on cannabis, but considerably sharper. I have just replayed the video of one of his two Quest excerpts. There were many passages of equal or greater intellectual interest, but I choose this one for a reason I shall disclose. Here is the transcript.

AC: Death – I think it's the greatest chance a person has of asserting his faith while everything else goes, mind or memory flee. Well, that's what we're all approaching, the subtraction of all our faculties; and yet this initial thing, faith, like a grain of sand, remains. I would love to think that death could be an offering of death to God, the supreme act of faith that is open to mankind. In view of the falling away of all you've ever known by the incarnate life, all of the falling away from you, and still, still, this extraordinary assertion that you believe in God, and that into his hands you are still commending your spirit.

IM: Can you translate that to the planet now facing the possibility of an end to history? Is our position that we should offer the planet to God in a resigned way, or should we struggle against its destruction?

AC: Unequivocally, in two sentences. One, we're all the more urged to stop the destruction of this world if we can, because quite obviously God's primary will in the matter is the salvation of the world. But also I was brought up in the Borders with a belief in the drastic strain in the Biblical teaching about God and the interpretation of history which one can reach legitimately in the light of what the Bible teaches, and I don't believe we can exclude the possibility, making a highly anthropomorphic statement, that God's patience snaps and allows the end to happen. That's the teaching and feeling of the second Psalm before the Hallelujah Chorus.

IM: But that's the Old Testament. Does God's patience snap after the Resurrection?

AC: That is really the key question. Did God insinuate his own being so deeply into the very heart of this incarnate and materialised world that we know of, that we can't contemplate His patience snapping? That's the key question.

IM: And your answer?

AC: I swither. I swither.

I would like now to replay that passage, as it were in actuality, because in synchronicity with the words there was something taking place which after four decades of broadcasting I see as one of the most remarkable *tours de force* I have witnessed. As he said '... all you've ever known', his gesturing arm knocked over the tumbler of water on the table beside him. Hesitation, even for a second, would have broken the viewer's concentration. But hesitation there was none. 'Still, still this extraordinary assertion', and he drew a hankie from his pocket.

As he spoke the words '... into his hands you are still commending your spirit', he was mopping the table and placing the glass upright.

No fresh take was needed. The flow of thoughts and words didn't falter; his eyes held us; the resonance of his spoken belief counterpointed the fluency of his movements with the calm interplay of a Brandenburg Concerto. A man who showed so little interest in controlling others controlled himself with meticulous grace – a clumsy phrase, but maybe it will do to indicate something beyond mind–body coordination, something like deep competence. Competence on the part of the Holy Spirit, and competent thinking on the part of those who seek to be guided in the Spirit. The Craig competence – I would say holy competence – was, despite what he said about the subtraction of faculties, so wonderfully undiminished that it is natural to ask what informed the wholeness of his thinking in the first place. An unusually accomplished, apparently *sui generis* horse still comes from a stable. Even if one had not already guessed, Archie betrayed something of the source of his balance in a quiet conversational diversion while others were busy with TV mechanics. He looked at me appraisingly, then poked at my professional armour. 'I think it's my turn to ask you a question. Tell me, how do you deal with theological balance in the BBC? What is your guiding principle, for example, vis-à-vis fundamentalist evangelicals?'

'Extreme prejudice', I said.

His eyes glittered. 'I am outraged. How can you, as a liberal-minded man representing a public interest, possibly defend a prejudice against a large and ever-growing religious position?'

'I can't defend it publicly. Privately I try to organise our limited resources in such a way that those who hijack God and corrupt language for narrow purposes do not finish up taking over the airwaves.'

There was quite a pause. 'Interesting', he said, and added: 'D'you know, I think you could defend your position publicly without bringing God into it at all. The corruption of language might be sufficient grounds.' And he chuckled.

The classical, moderate, rational tributary in Reformed churchmanship (I am neither a theologian nor a historian, so don't press me on details) flowed into the lives of many at university through the Student Christian Movement. As a student, I avoided all the religious societies like the plague, regarding them as ghettoes in what should be an open intellectual environment. Then David Read came along as University Chaplain. He was to finish up in New York, but he was then known in Edinburgh as a strong preacher. Above all, he was a reasonable man, a big man in physique, humour and his inclusive approach to university life. He launched a traditional (dead species) Mission to Edinburgh University, and to plan it brought together not only signed-up Christians but a huge range of other staff and students, of whom I was one.

It was a large exercise in what would nowadays be called outreach, and it was fun. It didn't change my religious opinions, such as they were, or my inner life, but it introduced me to SCM thinking and SCM people, and what that did was to provide me with a whole context, a world context, for consideration of Christian issues and values, and a language in which to discuss them rationally. I was asked to edit the *Mission* newspaper, and this led me to my first encounter with the extreme prejudice of some evangelicals against openness. One of the missioners was a well-known Baptist minister who embarked on a personal mission to save my soul. What it felt like was that he wanted my scalp notched up on his theological fuselage. He hounded me in cafes and on street corners and in letters. His summing-up of my dire spiritual condition was expressed simply: 'when I read the *Mission* paper you edit, all I see is a giant question mark'.

To hear Archie Craig say at the end of his life 'I swither' was to feel bonded again to the values of open-ended exploration, not as an alternative to commitment but as a component in that commitment.

If there was a cumulative reason why Archie was revered by so many, I take it to be that he wore in a seamless robe the gifts of rationality, openness, intuition, tenderness and faith. Yet these were not necessarily the aspects of ministry that would win him the heart of the Kirk, for all that he became Moderator. Even as a relatively intelligent student, I suppose I felt 'SCM thinking' was for students and that adults would graduate to the real business of establishing the kingdom through impressive good works in the Kirk. So, when I went onto the SCM staff, first in Scotland, then as Study Secretary in London, I wasn't surprised that the attitude of most Scottish clergy was expressed in the question: when will you come back and do a proper job in a parish?

Maybe Archie Craig was, looking at his career in long-shot, backward in coming forward into the Kirk limelight. But in close-up, as observed in the privacy of Doune, he was in the front line of ratiocinating love. To complete the picture, I have to return to our preliminary conversation some months before filming.

Dr Craig's wife May understood nothing. Yet, in another way, she understood everything. Her bright sweetness towards us and him revealed that she knew she was loved by this man she had once known as Archie.

He told us two things about their relationship. He said: 'I have had to relearn the alphabet of love'. And then he said: 'I'm only still here to look after her. When she goes, I will go.'

A few weeks after filming, she died. Two days after that, he died. We filmed his funeral. The Church was packed with the great and the good. As the huge male sound gave voice to 'Rock of Ages', I felt a shift in the ground of my being.

Who am I to assess Archie Craig on the basis of two days near the end of his life? But if I did dare to convey my final impressions, they might go something like this. He didn't pursue honours (though he received some) because he saw human success for what it was, *sub specie aeternitatis*. He was no politician, nor a pulpit magician. His magic was that he looked the world in the eye, valued it, but did not worship it. Who does that remind one of?

Tom Fleming once said to me in an interview: 'I decided to become an actor, not a star.' In other words, the brilliance was to be hidden in the commitment; what was to be revealed was not himself, but truth. Archie Craig didn't make it to the top. He was the top.

IAN MACKENZIE

GEORGE FIELDEN MACLEOD

EDITOR'S PREAMBLE

I first heard of George MacLeod from my sister, who had attended something of a recruitment meeting for the newly founded Iona Community while a student at Oxford. On responding with enthusiasm, she had been taken aback to discover that it had no place for women. Ten years later, my husband – who was an instinctive feminist – felt a similar reaction when George was recruiting at New College. Nonetheless, we remained admirers of his vision and the power of his preaching. A natural hierarch, he stood somewhat uneasily within the Reformed tradition; it too, however, needs its diverse prophets.

I first heard of George MacLeod in Sydney, Australia, in 1948. This extraordinary Scottish churchman of distinguished bearing drew crowds to hear him challenge and disturb the complacency of the churches. He spoke with urgency and passion. He also described a living experiment currently based on a Scottish island.

Who was this man? A complex personality full of paradoxes. Soldier, pacifist; realist, mystic; action man, contemplative; rebel and establishment figure; arrogant and humble; an intensely private man who believed in community.

Born into a well-to-do family in Glasgow, he was sent to school at Winchester College in the south of England. There he daily imbibed the liturgy of morning and evening prayers in the chapel and was confirmed a member of the Church of England. In 1913, he entered Oriel College, Oxford, to study law. In 1914, aged 19, he enlisted in the Argyll and Sutherland Highlanders. He spent most of the next four years in the trenches of France. Here his capacity for leadership, rapport with all ranks, and courage were put to extended test.

Given his heritage of distinguished Highland ministers – five Moderators of the Church of Scotland, three Deans of the Chapel Royal, two Deans of the Thistle and three royal chaplains – it was not surprising, after the war, that he should abandon the law for the church.

After studies in New College, Edinburgh, and Union Theological Seminary in New York, he was briefly an assistant minister in St Giles, Edinburgh. In 1924, he was ordained by the Presbytery of Glasgow for work with the Toc H movement in Scotland. Notably, he resigned from the movement within two years when it was announced that Holy Communion as celebrated in Toc H was open to confirmed Anglicans only. George MacLeod, in an early stance on intercommunion, resented the exclusivism of the Anglicans and resigned in protest.

Already thought of as a possible 'rising star', he was appointed in 1926 to be Collegiate Minister in Edinburgh's west-end church of St Cuthbert. Thus began the phase of his career which was set on a conventional path. He soon became the brilliant young minister with trendy Edinburgh at his feet. His preaching was compelling, the pews were crowded. He was the eligible young bachelor in a fashionable church destined for a 'prominent pulpit'.

But this was a time, 1926–30, of social and political unrest. The general strike of 1926, the Wall Street crash, and rising unemployment. From an early age, George MacLeod had been aware of 'the two nations' and of his own privileged position. St Cuthbert's had an outreach mission in a deprived part of Edinburgh, the Freer Street Mission in Fountainbridge. Here he was confronted with, and offended by, poor housing and severe poverty on the very doorstep of his bourgeois kirk. He felt at home with the people of Freer Street and spent much time there. He soon discovered, however, that they felt 'St Cuthbert's is no' for the likes of us'. St Cuthbert's, for its part, was content to accept the poverty and social conditions of Freer Street as having 'aye been'.

George MacLeod was acutely conscious of the gap between the west end and Freer Street and of how his ministry was trapped in conventional forms. He had fashioned and discovered his extraordinary ability to communicate, to use words to move hearts and minds, and was now impatient for reform. He was a young man determined to go places; just where he was going was not clear. In 1930, at the peak of his popularity, with the world of ecclesiastical success before him, he resigned from St Cuthbert's to accept a call to be minister of Govan Parish Church in Glasgow, a historic parish church in gentle decline set in the heart of industrial Glasgow.

Maybe Govan did not recognise what it was getting in George MacLeod, nor did George foresee the outcome of his turbulent years there. For him, the time had come for a deliberate attempt to change the way the mission of a parish church was implemented. A bold experiment was required – and Govan, set in the midst of social and industrial decline, was the ideal place for such an experiment.

He had offered to accept the call to Govan on certain conditions, thus avoiding later struggles and providing himself with a cover which would allow future changes. The conditions were: a return to a territorial ministry; sufficient permanent staff; and that he should live within the parish on the top floor of the Pearce Institute adjacent to the church building. The Institute was to become an important component of the parish work, a centre for meetings, classes, social activities, a reading room and cheap nutritious food for the wider community.

So began a powerful drive, assisted by four full-time staff, to breathe life into the parish church and to engage with the men and institutions of the industrial life of the area. The programme included the door-to-door visitation of every home in the parish. New services of worship were offered, Holy Communion was celebrated each Sunday, ecumenical services were introduced – with Episcopal and Roman Catholic clergy participating – and pastoral care was a priority at all times. Youth organisations were re-energised, and the Pearce Institute became a place of engagement with employed and unemployed men and their families.

It was a cracking pace, but was it working? In January 1933, in spite of all the effort and the work of many good people, he was overcome by a feeling of hopeless depression. His father came to the rescue and took him away for a three-month journey of convalescence to the Holy Land. It was a journey which changed his life and the lives of many others.

It happened in Jerusalem at the early Easter morning service of the Russian Orthodox church. He later described it as an experience of almost perfect worship. He had rediscovered the church as the corporate Body of Christ.

> For George MacLeod, lukewarm conventional Presby-
> terianism finally died in the Holy Land on Easter Sunday
> 1933. The old structure of individual devotion and duty
> had cracked in the crucible that was Govan in the hungry
> thirties, and he knew in his heart of hearts that it could
> not be repaired by more work, or even by more faith. He
> needed for his healing a new way of *seeing*, and he found
> new vision in the midst of overwhelming, mysteriously
> beautiful worship. It was a vision which was personal,
> political and cosmic *all at the same time*, and it appealed
> to the Celt in him. Holiness had become wholeness had
> become holiness. It was as if the spiritual and the material
> fused in a never-to-be-forgotten rapturous moment of
> revelation. (from Ronald Ferguson, *George MacLeod*,
> Collins 1990, p. 110)

He returned to Govan with renewed energy, a new vision, intent on furthering the experiment. He was fortunate to have with him in his team, at various times, David Cairns, Hugh Douglas, John Symington, Isobel Rutherford, later to become Mrs Hugh Douglas, Harry Whitely and others. A two-year plan of mission was announced. A programme of street preaching was undertaken, and invitations to debate with communists, atheists and others were never refused. The programmes at the Pearce Institute were busier than ever.

Increasingly dissatisfied with the traditional form of Presbyterian worship, he introduced congregational said-responses, kneeling to pray, ecumenical services and weekly celebration of Holy Communion. Accused of Roman Catholic practices, he claimed he was recovering the genuine catholic insights of the Reformers. 'Recover' was one of his favourite words, frequently used to justify a new initiative or experiment.

The services of public worship were well attended. The BBC broadcast services from Govan for listeners at home as well as worldwide – the beginning of George MacLeod's recognition that he could use the new media of radio and television to communicate effectively to many audiences. He did so famously over the following five decades.

Early in 1935, a small discovery presaged another experiment. Fingalton Mill was a ruin on the edge of Fenwick Moor, less than fifteen miles from Govan. Here was an opportunity. Rebuild the mill, invite unemployed tradesmen to restore it as a holiday and conference centre for the people of Govan. The men gave their time and skills willingly and were proud of their achievement. Opened in June 1935, it became an outlet in the country for families, a place for conference, discovery and refreshment – a place, too, where boys from Polmont Reformatory were brought for 'a week's experience' in a freer atmosphere. Here, as a by-product, ministers found themselves working alongside tradesmen, doing the chores with families, mixing with Borstal boys.

Here were the seeds of ideas later to emerge in the rebuilding on Iona, the setting-up of the Camas camp in an old fishing station on the Ross of Mull, and ultimately the establishment of Community House in the heart of Glasgow.

Other forces were about. The industrial strength of the area was crumbling, unemployment was endemic, poverty was widespread and housing was unbelievably bad. There was precious little sign of the new age many had hoped for after the First World War. George MacLeod was deeply affected by the social and political injustice so evident in Govan and so well exposed by the communists and others. He respected their sincerity and commitment, and found himself and his team arguing, debating, persuading that there was a better way and that Christianity held the key.

At this time, he was influenced by Archbishop William Temple and the Reverend Dick Sheppard. Temple's emphasis was on the incarnation, arguing 'that since God had taken on human flesh in love for the world, all of life was sacred and under the rule of Christ. Unemployment and poverty were therefore offences not just against man but against God.' Dick Sheppard at St Martin in the Fields in London was energetically trying to make Christianity meaningful, and transformed St Martin's into a vibrant centre of mission. Meanwhile, George MacLeod was moving for the first time to a pacifist position. He signed up with Dick Sheppard's Peace Pledge Union.

The Govan experiment was seemingly a success: well-attended services of worship, intensive pastoral care, a parish mission strategy, lively youth organisations and a team of enthusiastic church staff keen to change the world – all in all, an experiment widely admired and copied.

George MacLeod was not so sure. He felt that, while the church had 'the answer', it was not 'getting through'. Maybe, just maybe, the church itself was the problem. What was required was a living experiment in community, a communal expression of the Christian faith. Once again, at the point when the world proclaimed 'Success!', he resigned, aged 42, in April 1938 and set out to attempt another experiment, this time on the island of Iona, the island of St Columba.

Why Iona? The answer is not clear. He knew the island well. His family had holidayed there, he had shared divinity student Easter retreats there, and the buildings had always seemed to him to cry out to be rebuilt. David Russell of Markinch, Fife, had investigated the possibility of restoration and had commissioned a scheme and put it, without result, to the Cathedral Trustees in 1933. George MacLeod was aware of the proposal and in 1935 contributed to a further proposal, partly to counter what he considered to be an inappropriate scheme put forward by an American group. At that time, it seems he had no intention of being personally involved with the implementation of a scheme; but in 1938 he made a firm proposal to the Iona Cathedral Trustees to restore the living quarters of the Abbey and to combine this with a living experiment in the training of ministers. This time, he offered personally to lead the experiment and to be responsible for the finances as well as the costs of the restoration undertaken. The proposal was accepted.

Why? A passionate conviction that new insights and ways had to be found to be the church and to carry out its mission? The tug of Iona, an island inherent with sanctity, rich in Celtic and Benedictine history? An abbey church waiting to be a vibrant centre of reformed worship? A place where a brotherhood, a fellowship, a Christian community could be established? A place of spiritual refreshment from which, as in Columban times, ministers and laymen could go throughout Scotland and beyond to serve the church of Christ in new ways – yet to be explored?

It was a vision and a huge personal risk. Where was the money to come from? Who would want to participate in the experiment? As serious a gamble, however, was that he embarked on this experiment with all its implications without the support or authority of a Presbytery, without 'official' approval. 'The Church of Scotland woke up to find there was an exciting and bewildering new show in town – revamped Presbyterianism in Celtic drag, with Catholic song and dance routines – and it was going to run and run, whether they liked it or not' (Ferguson, p. 154).

He persuaded a group of well-trusted senior churchmen, including John and Donald Baillie, John White, David S. Cairns and Charles Warr, to act as 'Sponsors' as a form of legitimation for the project. Thus it was that in the summer of 1938 the embryonic community arrived on the island to begin the experiment with their own lives. There were six young ministers, six craftsmen, a doctor, a secretary, an architect and George MacLeod. The rest is history.

After a difficult survival during the war, the idea of the community captured the imagination and conviction of more young ministers. On joining the Iona Community, they spent three summer months living in the Abbey (originally in a hut in the grounds of the Abbey). They acted as unskilled labourers to the craftsmen – joiners, slaters, masons, electricians and others. On alternate days, time was given for the study of ministerial craftsmanship – Bible study, lectures, discussions and planning future work on the mainland. The programme examined alternative forms of ministry and experiments being carried out in other churches, for example house churches, worker priests, industrial missions, healing ministries and different forms of parish mission, all with an overarching emphasis on engagement with the social and political issues of the day.

All of this was set within a framework, Monday to Saturday, of morning and evening worship in the Abbey while living and working together with the craftsmen and the sharing of all the mundane chores of a living community. It was a heady mix.

At the end of the three summer months on Iona, the new member-ministers were required to work for two years as probationers, or apprentices, attached to an existing minister-member in a parish or with an experiment elsewhere. After the two years, a new member was expected, but not compelled, to go into work as a parish minister in a downtown difficult area or in a new housing area, or to work in industrial mission or a full-time experiment in another church or movement, for example at Peckham in London, or to serve in the mission of the church overseas.

During and after the two years' training, members of the Iona Community had the ever-ready support of fellow members, bi-monthly meetings of all members (i.e. those in the UK), local family-group meetings as well as visits from staff, for example Ralph Morton, Penry Jones or George MacLeod. All of this amounted to a practical training and support scheme which the Divinity Colleges or Presbyteries had wholly failed to provide.

All members of the Iona Community were individually committed to observe the personal discipline known as 'The Daily Rule' – shades of a monastic 'Rule'. This included daily Bible-reading, prayers for members, prayers for specific concerns, and planning the use of one's time and money. This was another of George MacLeod's experiments presented as a 'recovery' of best practice.

It is not surprising that the members of the Iona Community were regarded by some as a suspect 'movement' within the church, a dangerous task force committed to finding and practising new ways to engage with the changing social, political and spiritual conditions of the day – often seen as a threat to the establishment or as agents of Roman Catholicism or as irresponsible socialist revolutionaries or even as the personal agents of George MacLeod.

Ever a man of paradox, there was, however, a fateful trace in his make-up from his Victorian upbringing regarding women. Women were not a part of his vision for the Iona Community. Many found his attitude narrow-minded if not offensive. After he retired, Dr Nancy Brash became the first woman member. In 2002, the Reverend Kathy Galloway was appointed as the first female Leader of the Community.

Iona was the summer place of gathering, training and refreshment while the real work was undertaken on the mainland or abroad. In Govan, the Pearce Institute was an important base for classes, debates and all sorts of meetings. George MacLeod saw the need for a similar experiment as a base for the Iona Community on the mainland, preferably in industrial Glasgow. A property was acquired at 214 Clyde Street, Glasgow, which as Community House became a lively place to meet all sorts and conditions of people, a place where anyone could 'drop in', use the cafeteria, participate in classes, plan campaigns, debate current social and political issues or just seek help. Everyone entering Community House knew that this was a Christian place engaging with worldly issues. From here, the Industrial Mission work of the Iona Community was first developed in the shipyards and engineering works of Glasgow and the Clyde.

George MacLeod's influence and the work of the Iona Community spread throughout the world. Many came to look and learn, and young men from other countries and churches applied to join the Community.

From his time as an assistant in St Giles, Edinburgh, at Toc H, Freer Street and in Govan, George MacLeod had always understood the importance of work with young people. Was not Iona an ideal place for another experiment? A Youth Secretary was appointed to organise and lead summer camps for young people on Iona. Young people came from all over Scotland and beyond for a week's holiday. Accommodated under canvas or in huts, they attended morning and evening worship in the Abbey, a programme of discussions, sharing the chores and plenty of recreational time. These camps were immensely popular and led to many young people becoming active in their local churches and becoming future leaders in church and society. A special camp was established in an old salmon station at Camas on the Ross of Mull.

George MacLeod was a man of deep personal devotion. He was wont to spend hours alone on his knees, struggling in prayer to seek light, guidance, strength and forgiveness. Here he found the deep springs which inspired and fed his public activity.

To be led in public worship in Iona Abbey by George MacLeod was to experience the moving fullness of worship. This ancient place of worship, a place where 'the boundaries are wafer-thin', a place inherent with sanctity, became numinous, holy, spiritual and revelatory. The whole liturgy would be meticulously prepared – the music, the participants, the readings, prayers and sermon – all designed as a single whole.

George MacLeod was a true seer. He saw things others didn't. He saw further into things. He saw into the past and into the future. He saw into souls. He was human, of course. Over issues big and small he could be petty, blind, deaf, stubborn. But on the whole, in him was as clear an access to the Word made flesh as I'm likely to meet. And as many thousands would attest, one met it closest in worship and specially in the conduct of Holy Communion. When, leading up to the breaking of the bread, he spoke the Great Prayer, the central part of which he spent hours writing fresh for every Sunday, the earth moved. And heaven moved. And in some way they fused. It wasn't just inspiring, it was shattering. An extra presence, a boundary crossed. A transubstantiation of matter and spirit in dangerous fission and fusion. As his stupendous words mounted into a climax of clashing metaphor, it really was as if Christ was released in an explosion of light-energy. We can't compute how many lives were altered by that experience. (Ian Mackenzie, in *The Scottish Review*, Spring 2002)

In September 1967, he resigned as Leader, aged 72. The Community which he had begun as a small, risky experiment twenty-nine years previously was now an established institution in its own right, responsible for its own direction. It was time for fresh leadership.

In 1951, the Iona Community, after many struggles, had been brought within the jurisdiction of the Church of Scotland. The move was from the periphery to the centre. In the years to come, George played a prominent part in the affairs and committees of the Church of Scotland. He was elected to be Moderator of the General Assembly for the year 1957. His greatest moments were in the annual debates of the General Assembly. In his closing address as Moderator in 1957, he spoke passionately in support of the so-called Bishop's Report (proposing *inter alia* bishops in Presbytery), pleading for patience as the church considered the report, and equally passionately against the production and use of nuclear bombs.

At the time of the proposed Central African Federation, in 1959, he introduced against strong opposition the (then) radical motion 'that effective power be given to the African community in Nyasaland' and persuaded the Assembly to agree. The government took notice.

For many years, he introduced motions in the Assembly against nuclear weapons. It was almost a set-piece. A passionate speech was assured. Each year, the Assembly failed to support him, but he returned again the following year. In 1986, in his ninety-first year, he proposed: 'As of now, this General Assembly declares that no church can accede to the use of nuclear weapons to defeat any cause whatever. They call on Her Majesty's government to desist from their use and stop their further development.' He sat down. No speech. His traditional opponent said the time had come for him to agree with Dr MacLeod. The Assembly voted almost unanimously to support the motion. After all these years, George had seen victory.

In 1967, he was made a life peer: Lord MacLeod of Fuinary, the first Church of Scotland minister to sit in the House of Lords. He sat on the cross benches, where he said he got crosser and crosser. He found himself somewhat adrift among their Lordships. In 1990, he was awarded the prestigious Templeton Prize given for outstanding contribution to the development of religion.

In Govan, he had moved to a position of pacifism which he maintained throughout the Second World War. In his later years, it became a dominant theme. He never tired of campaigning in this cause or of persuading people to sign postcards in support. For him, nuclear weapons were an abuse of the atom, 'the living material a blasphemy against the holy at the heart of the universe'.

An ecumenist all his days, he became increasingly disillusioned with more and more 'conversations', 'papers' and 'dialogues'. His instinct was for action, for experiment, for sharing the eucharist. He had always revelled in the terms of the Duke of Argyll's gift of Iona Abbey to the Trustees (themselves Church of Scotland) that members of churches, other than the Church of Scotland, should be allowed to hold services in the Abbey. From time to time, he encouraged the celebration of the eucharist in the Abbey by Anglican and Roman Catholic clergy. He believed that the way to unity was by faithful experiment.

George MacLeod, nearly blind, remained urgent to the end, which came in 1991. He was a paradox of a man, elusive and not without flaws: a man with flair and great humility, a passionate campaigner, prophet, priest, pastor and disciple – a great churchman. His life was given to the working-out of obedience to that life-changing cosmic vision of 1933 in Jerusalem.

Ross Flockhart

ROBERT MACKIE

EDITOR'S PREAMBLE

Robert Mackie was very much the father of the SCM in my time, indeed of all things ecumenical in Scotland, although always as the enabler in the background. When circumstances made it impossible for Jean Fraser, his erstwhile WCC colleague and later Principal of St Colm's College, to continue with his projected biography, I was happy to take over the project. *In Love and in Laughter*, published by Saint Andrew Press in 1995, was the result. My work was made all the more intriguing by the open access given by Steven Mackie to his father's papers, which include his letters and diaries.

Most of the subjects in this current book naturally knew one another; but one of the closest friendships was between Robert Mackie and Archie Craig, as they shared a similar temperament and sense of humour.

At the occasion of the reunion of the Church of Scotland and the United Free Church in 1929, Robert Mackie wrote:

> the really important things still happen in the streets of Edinburgh where everyone can see. I stood opposite the house where Burns once lived in the Lawnmarket, and every window ... had faces in it. We were all waiting for the 'processions'. Slowly, almost silently, with no pomp and circumstance, they came. The 'Auld Kirk' came down the Lawnmarket, and the 'U.F.' came up from the Mound. They were long columns of black-coated ministers and elders – old men who had known the bitterness of religious controversy in Scotland, and young men who had been at Swanwick or Moffat [SCM conference events] a year or two ago. In a high wind, for Edinburgh did its characteristic best for the occasion, the two columns met in the High Street and marched four abreast to the High Kirk. As Moderator bowed and shook hands with Moderator, as minister and elder greeted the men whom chance had brought along the street to be their companions, the crowd began to sing. There in that place which has seen most of Scotland's history, often a sad history, where men have marched singing to their death for conscience' sake, the words and notes of the old psalms hung lingeringly among the crow-stepped gables, and passed up into the windy sky above the crown of St Giles.

On 21st September 2001, we spilled out of St Giles again into the Lawnmarket – the 400 official delegates to the first Scottish Ecumenical Assembly – to march under banners together, women and men, young and old, lay and clerical, committed by our churches to hammer out, under the general theme of 'Breaking New Ground', a five-year ecumenical agenda for cooperation over the problems of church and society – problems brought into immediate and stark focus by the events in New York on the 11th. The difference now was that the participants were not merely from two divisions of Scottish Presbyterianism but from the whole range of divided denominations in Scotland. They included the nine members of Action of Churches Together in Scotland – the Church of Scotland, Congregationalist Federation, Methodist Church, Religious Society of Friends, Roman Catholic Church, Salvation Army, Scottish Episcopal Church, United Free Church of Scotland and United Reformed Church.

No one person was more responsible for this ecumenical advance in Scotland than Robert Mackie. After he returned to Scotland from his work as General Secretary of the World Student Christian Federation and first Associate General Secretary of the World Council of Churches from 1938 to 1955, he was described as 'perhaps the best-known Scot outside Scotland'. This was reiterated by Archie Craig at the time of his death in 1984: 'The mature Robert was a world figure exerting a width and weight and quality of Christian influence unwielded by any other Scottish minister of religion for decades past'.

He was born in 1899, the son of the United Presbyterian minister to Bothwell, a small town ten miles south of Glasgow. After a brief but challenging experience of leadership of battle-worn troops at the end of the First World War and an influential period as chaplain to the Jharia Coalfield in India, Robert found his vocation in the climate of change and disillusionment of post-war Britain. Looking back in 1982, he wrote:

> the immediate world concern that really affected my generation was the discovery that our European fellow students – in Russia, in Eastern Europe and in Germany – were in deep poverty and distress. There was a crowded meeting in the Union to decide whether we should take part in European Student Relief. ... This was a challenge which it was not easy to meet after the bitterness of war. Gradually there arose a new sense of solidarity with our fellow students. We went round business premises asking

for … surplus clothing. To the Glasgow 1921 Conference we each brought an extra pair of shoes to send to … European Student Relief. In our own University we found overseas students widened our horizons. I well remember a Chinese medical student startling a small group in active discussion by saying: 'The trouble about you people is that you cannot escape from your Christian background!' We realised suddenly the limits of our experience and the weakness of our judgements. We had so much to learn.

This realisation was to remain with Robert, and the capacity to learn was his to the end of his days. And from such simple beginnings came the outstanding Director of Inter-Church Aid at the World Council of Churches.

With the accelerating pace of secularisation, and a decreasing historical sensitivity, it is difficult in the twenty-first century to appreciate the impact of the Student Christian Movement on British universities from the foundation of the World Student Federation in 1895. Indeed, by 1935 its official membership stood at 11,500 out of a total student population of 72,000 – and this did not include the many participants in study groups, meetings and conferences who do not figure in the records, as, from conviction, all events were of an open nature. This conviction followed from an explicit commitment to the 'student vocation', to the search for truth and the spirit of enquiry. Not surprisingly, therefore, the SCM proved responsive to the times – to radicalism in both scholarship and politics. Explicitly Christian in character, it did not confuse its function with that of churches, much less of sects, and refused to set doctrinal tests for members. Thus it included in its ranks a genuine cross-section of the university community (including faculty), from high Anglicans to Baptists and Barthians. It has taken the churches a long time to catch up – where they have – in many areas, such as the acceptance of the centrality of the 'laity', the parity of women and men, the demands of ecumenism, the fruits of biblical criticism, and the primacy of the world's need on the Christian agenda. Randall Davidson, then Archbishop of Canterbury, said of the SCM in 1927: 'Organisation is too rigid and prosaic a word to describe a movement which in its spontaneity and buoyancy, its international character and its quiet force seems to me one of the most remarkable movements which any part of Christendom at any place or time has seen'. In a deeply symbiotic relationship, Robert Mackie exercised in Scotland and then further afield in Britain the essential but rare qualities of leadership that such a unique organisation required: interpreter, mediator, enabler (before the word became fashionable).

This was recognised by Robert Mackie's colleagues at the time. Eric Duncan wrote: 'Robert, more than anyone else I have ever known, emerged triumphantly from all the conferences, committees, minute drafting, project initiating, clarifying of others' muddled thoughts, at all of which he was such a master – emerged as a sensitive, profoundly understanding human being. Once in Geneva Visser 't Hooft said to me in some astonishment, "Robert says he doesn't like administration! That is absurd! It's like Rembrandt saying he doesn't like painting!"'

Speakers used by the SCM in the 1930s reflected the nature of the times and included C. F. Andrews, John and Donald Baillie, Dietrich Bonhoeffer, Cecil of Chelwood, Archie Craig, C. H. Dodd, T. S. Eliot, Wilfred Grenfell, C. S. Lewis, Donald Mackinnon, John Macmurray, Karl Mannheim, George MacLeod, John Middleton Murry, John R. Mott, Lesslie Newbigin, Reinhold Niebuhr, Martin Niemoller, D. T. Niles, J. H. Oldham, Michael Polanyi, Dorothy Sayers, Albert Schweitzer, William Temple, K. H. Ting and Visser 't Hooft.

Robert, however, always remained wary of the large gathering; this was, after all, the decade of the Nuremberg rallies and the Hitler Youth movement. He describes a WSCF meeting at Bad Boll in 1932:

> It was glorious spring weather, and we often sat in a wide circle in the garden ... [by] a highway along which groups of singing young people passed incessantly. Many carried banners – some with Christian symbols, some with Communist, some with national socialist symbols. As we read our Bibles and discussed the Gospel we were pledged to proclaim, we could not keep our eyes off this stream of young people. Where were they going? Where was Europe going? Where were we going? I have a vivid memory of our closing worship. It was led by Reinhold von Thadden and by Pierre Maury.

The former was German SCM leader and in 1936 one of the ten signatories of the document sent by the Confessing Church to Hitler challenging Nazi ideology and practice in the name of the gospel, for which he was arrested by the Gestapo. Field Commander of Louvain during its German occupation, he had the unique distinction of being honoured by its citizens after the war for the protection he had afforded them. Pierre Maury, on the other hand, was leader of the French SCM. His son, Philippe, active in the French Resistance during the war, became Robert Mackie's successor as WSCF General Secretary in 1948. It is not surprising, with such personal contacts, that SCM members in different countries developed, earlier than most, a sense of solidarity with the world church and, consequently, provided many of the first generations of ecumenical leaders.

It was under Robert's leadership that the Study Department of the British SCM in 1937 launched an innovative type of conference based on the study-group method. 'Right action springs from true thinking', he wrote. Reading lists were sent out ahead of time, a library was assembled, preparation was required from everyone, and the occasional lecture by figures of some distinction was only in the nature of stimulation. The whole event lasted for ten days. Significantly, it proved easy to recruit both junior and senior participants – often serious enquirers on the frontiers of faith who avoided didactic preaching like the plague. This venture continued for a decade or so after the Second World War but has been too little emulated by the churches; lay theological training has developed in rather different ways on the 'open college' model. I still admit, however, to a certain shock when a conference session labelled 'Bible Study' turns out to be a lecture by a cleric.

An initiative from these 'Depression' years which has had more obvious successors, in terms of industrial chaplaincies (possibly a clerical and institutional sub-version?), was the Industrial Department, a good example of 'the world setting the agenda'. The 'ideas' man was Edwin Barker, SCM Industrial Secretary; but little could have been done without Robert's encouragement. By 1936, the Department had held one International, two British and fifty local conferences, work camps and action committees, variously including employers, trade unions, the unemployed, economists, farmers, technical students and theologians.

The official establishment of the World Council of Churches was delayed by the Second World War in 1939, but a provisional committee was set up in order to preserve the impetus of the ecumenical process which had gathered strength and scope since the Edinburgh World Mission Conference in 1910. There was considerable agreement in the choice of first General Secretary, Visser 't Hooft, General Secretary of the WSCF since 1932. He, however, was so convinced that the churches were as yet dependent on the WSCF's ecumenical network, particularly in the light of the imminence of war, that he reportedly refused to accept the appointment unless Robert agreed to succeed him at the WSCF. Thus, in 1938, Robert moved with his family to a base in Geneva. Aware that war would curtail most movement, he immediately set out to visit as many threatened SCMs as possible in the time left, including

Czechoslovakia, which was full of a sense of betrayal by the actions of Britain and France. From the International Missionary Council in Madras, his wife, Dorothy, wrote: 'It is amazing how these lads just fall on Robert like a long-lost brother and don't want to let him out of their sight'. There was a particular closeness between the British and Indian SCMs, with Gandhi, as it were, the Mandela of the day.

After Singapore, Robert visited 'free' China in Kunming, the home of three displaced universities, then international China in Hong Kong and Shanghai, then occupied China in Peiping – all this by the most primitive forms of transport for economy's sake. Then he went to Korea, also occupied by Japan, and to Japan itself, where he found himself 'interpreting silences', aware of the risks taken willingly by others for the sake of his presence. Finally, he made a comprehensive tour of North America from Vancouver through Texas, New York and back to Montreal, always sustaining and developing contacts which were the lifeblood of the Federation.

On his return to Geneva, he was immediately absorbed in the organisation of the World Conference of Christian Youth – in preparation since 1935, and held in Amsterdam in July 1939. It was decided the time had come within the ecumenical movement to face the division over the sacrament of communion, previously ignored. A version of the model then introduced has since become frequently used. Full eucharistic services in the Anglican, Lutheran, Orthodox and Reformed traditions were held and all invited to attend, but only in the latter case to communicate. The most difficult task of leading a joint introductory service was given to Robert; recollections of the occasion reverberated in ecumenical circles for many years. He said:

> In this place we ought all to be one because we ought to be one Christian family. But we have failed ... Remember.

It is the Lord's Supper. Jesus Christ is the host ... It is not our Communion that is broken – it is the body of our Lord Jesus Christ that is broken. And for that we must ask forgiveness. And yet – and this is the real miracle – He comes to our divided communion as Host. He takes our divided bread, and blesses, and breaks and gives. Whoever of us will be absent from any one of our communion services, Jesus Christ will be there.

On 3rd September war was declared. Until the war finished, so that church contacts might be maintained across frontiers, and by overt and covert means, Visser 't Hooft and Robert based themselves in Geneva and Toronto respectively. Robert was able to use *The Student World* – the Federation's periodical, of which he was editor – as an influential means of communication. Its volumes provide a valuable archival record of Christian opinion over the period. He also took the opportunity to make pioneering visits to South America and the Caribbean, on which others were later able to build. Another urgent task was the raising of resources to help student refugees and prisoners of war. As soon as possible after the end of hostilities, he visited Germany and Czechoslovakia, and Federation colleagues worked in China and South-East Asia. He headed a magnificent team, all of whom paid tribute to his skills in the period of reconciliation and reconstruction. The young Philip Potter, later to be Visser 't Hooft's successor at the WCC, then newly arrived from Jamaica, watched him deal with a series of crises and wrote: 'I thought of the person of Barnabas in the Acts of the Apostles, the one who encouraged and enabled people ... there were a lot of sores that were still open and those of us who came from ... the third world were in a very militant mood'.

In 1948, Robert gave a classic statement on the per-ennially contested subject of the relationship between Christianity and politics:

We are fully aware that some readers think that we should avoid the discussion of politics in the pages of *The Student World*, and indeed in the Federation itself. This argument is based on the truth that as Christians we are primarily concerned with the Gospel. Now let us freely admit that political discussion may be a way of escaping from the demands of Jesus Christ upon our lives. But so indeed may be worship and Bible study and evangelism. Any human activity may provide an excuse for avoiding a face-to-face encounter with our Lord ... When we try to keep our politics separate from our religion, and out of our movements, it usually means that our political opinions will not stand the full light of the Gospel upon them ... We know now, or we ought to know, that the interaction of different forms of power makes policy. We influence the future more by the food we eat, and the freedom on which we insist, than by the opinions we pronounce or the advice we offer to public men. We are caught in the machinery of power and it is there that we must act as Christians. Any separation of our faith and worship from this entanglement of our lives is like creating pleasant gardens round a factory without concern as to whether it is manufacturing for the essential needs of men or for their destruction.

With considerable misgivings, Robert Mackie accepted the combined role of Associate General Secretary to the WCC and Director of its Department of Inter-Church Aid in 1948. No-one knew better that the aftermath of war had escalated the overwhelming demands on the latter. He was concerned that there should be even-handed assessment of needs, be it in China or the Balkans. The Orthodox had been involved in the ecumenical process since before the First World War, and he had always been sensitive to their particular situation. It was at his urging, therefore, that the WCC in 1950 issued a recommendation: 'The Central Committee recognises that there are Churches in Europe and in particular Orthodox Churches, which do not have sister Churches of the same communion to help them. It, therefore, asks all contributing Churches to set aside and place at the disposal of the Department some portion of their giving for this ecumenical service across confessional lines.' A Romanian Orthodox leader wrote to Robert: 'As a minister of Christ you have been the main channel through which the parable of the Good Samaritan was applied on a very large scale. In the whole history of Christianity, for the first time, Christian Churches of the West have been wonderful in doing as much as they could in helping their fellow brethren, who lost everything but their faith in God and in their fellow-men'. A similar concern for the preservation of church unity lay behind the foundation of the Conference of European Churches in the 1950s. Unfortunately, over time, the resurgence of international confessionalism has rather undermined this self-denying ordinance. In the 1980s, the current Bishop of Hanover, responding to my appreciation of the low-profile, non-directive generosity of the West German churches to poorer members of the Conference of European Churches, said they had learned the right way to help from Robert's example to them in the aftermath of war.

Robert decided to return to Scotland in 1955 to a chorus of regret and appreciation from friends and colleagues around the world, perhaps best summed up by one: 'More than most of us realise, you have served as a kind of ecumenical cement, to hold together the galaxy of primates and prima donnas who adorn the World Council fellow-ship. You have done much to humanize the rarefied atmosphere ... your greatest contribution has been to help provide the ecumenical movement with a heart'.

It is entirely characteristic, therefore, that for another thirty years he exercised the same type of leadership – but in one small country, his own – with little reward or status, because ecumenism was peripheral to existing church structures. For nearly twenty of those years, he also nursed his increasingly ailing wife with devotion and sensitivity, devising – like his friend Archie Craig – a secure, loving and joyful daily routine for one with a confused grip on reality. In 2002, Ian Fraser concluded that Robert Mackie was the mainspring of most Scottish ecumenical activity during this period. He facilitated more efficient cooperative structures between diverse and sometimes dysfunctional organisations of both an official and unofficial nature, working towards the establishment of a new Scottish Council of Churches in 1964. He chaired the Executive of the 'Tell Scotland' movement and the planning committee of Aberdeen Kirk Week in 1957. The latter was in some ways an indigenous version of the German post-war Kirchentag and an alternative to the nineteenth-century mission-rally approach. It re-emphasised the centrality of lay leadership and the lay vocation, involving every aspect of the life of the city from the Lord Provost down. (Many of the emphases inherent in such activities have, thankfully, been rediscovered in the acceptance of the *Church without Walls* Report by the General Assembly in 2001.) Ian, who was first Warden, considers that the purchase and imaginative reconstruction of Scottish Churches' House from the Dunblane Cathedral cottages would never have been achieved without Robert's persistence and persuasion. It is ecumenically owned and a visible symbol of church unity.

Always he remained 'on call' as the World and British Council of Churches' troubleshooter and – Archie Craig's phrase – 'the world's best chairman': Hungary, Beirut, Central Africa, New Delhi; a senior statesman who was never too busy to help out in small local parishes. An early colleague, Kay Fenn, spoke truly when she said of Robert: 'He went through the world expecting the son of God to pass'.

NANSIE BLACKIE

ISOBEL FORRESTER

EDITOR'S PREAMBLE

I first met Isobel Forrester as my hostess in the autumn of 1947 – one of the 'countless visitors' of whom Ray Baxter writes. I was new on the Scottish SCM staff and to the Scottish university scene, having just left Lady Margaret Hall, Oxford, her own old college, so I needed to learn a lot quickly. She was of the greatest help, being a key figure on the ecumenical scene. The household included a very bright ten-year-old, called Duncan.

I remember the particular charm of the Dollarbeg conferences over which Isobel presided. Of course you had to sing for your supper, so I was paired off as a speaker with the immensely charismatic Father John Groser, who exercised a remarkable ministry in London's east end. He was a striking, prophetic figure with long white hair – younger, of course, than I am now.

It took me some time to realise that women in the Church of Scotland of Isobel's generation – and indeed of my own – inhabited a sort of 'shadow church' of women's organisations, being so marginalised by the official structures. This had not been my experience as an expatriate Scot in the Presbyterian Church of England nor, above all, in the SCM. This was, in some ways, made worse by the ambiguous category of 'minister's wife' – of which I myself was to have some experience a few years later.

Life & Work, November 1976:

> Mrs Isobel Forrester, who died recently, was widely known as a leader of the ecumenical movement in Scotland. A daughter of the Free Church Manse in Glenlyon, Isobel McColl won a scholarship to Lady Margaret Hall, Oxford, and was general secretary of the Girls' Auxiliary of the UF Church, to which her father had adhered at the cost of eviction. She later married W. R. Forrester, who held the St Andrews chair of Practical Theology and Christian Ethics from 1935 to 1958.

My first meeting with Isobel Forrester was in 1949 as her daughter's friend, newly arrived from London to work in Scotland. I was quickly made to feel part of the family. Later, I came to know Isobel as President of the Women's Foreign Mission Committee and as one of the leading members of the Scottish ecumenical movement. I vividly remember the Forrester home in St Andrews. Isobel fulfilled her role as wife and mother of five children, and as hostess to countless visitors. In her kitchen, she exercised a pastoral role for generations of students, and for them she was a great enabler. She and her husband would entertain others for Sunday tea. This would be a chance to tell people of her concerns for some of the missionaries with whom she was in touch and of introducing them to a great variety of people from home and overseas. I can still hear the enthusiasm in her voice as she spoke of the people who would lead the next ecumenical conference.

Before her marriage, Isobel McColl had wanted to be an overseas missionary. As the first from her Edinburgh school to gain a scholarship to Oxford, she studied there during the First World War. On her return to Scotland, as General Secretary of the Girls' Auxiliary of the Women's Foreign Mission Committee of the United Free Church, she exercised the vigorous leadership which was to characterise her whole life. The main function of the GA was to educate girls and young women about the life and work of overseas mission. By the time of their Jubilee celebrations in 1951, they were supporting up to twelve women working overseas. After the 1929 Union of the churches, the Girls' Auxiliary and the Girls' Guild of the Church of Scotland joined to form the Girls' Association. Education took the shape of annual Bible Conferences at Bonskeid and local Bible Study groups. Training and information was given in the GA magazine *The Trailmaker*. Support was, in the first place, financial, but for Isobel it always included using her intellectual and teaching gifts to help produce training material and Bible Study outlines. As well as this, she kept in personal touch with GA members and missionaries, exercising that 'quality of loving that does not dry up'. In all her later work with the Women's Foreign Mission (WFM) Committee of the Church of Scotland, and the Ecumenical Committee and Association, she continued to be pastor, enabler and educator.

Her spheres of ministry were in her home, in work with women and girls, with overseas missionaries and in the ecumenical movement. This involved a great deal of training, publicising and supporting. Her work as manse wife in Roslin and Gorgie included training Sunday School superintendents and teachers.

As far back as 1927, the Youth Committees of the Church of Scotland and the United Free Church of Scotland published her 'Everyday letters to a Sunday School Superintendent – Imaginary Correspondence on the Work of a Preparation Class'. For many years, she edited the *Sunday School Primary Quarterly* with notes on Bible passages and suggestions for the conduct of worship and practical Sunday School work.

As WFM President, at the end of the Second World War, Isobel Forrester made sure that the women at home and all concerned with mission were informed about the countries in which missionaries served and the life they led.

She recognised the loneliness of female missionaries and kept in touch with them, not only when they were abroad but also when they were home on leave or retired. People still remember her Prayer Letters and Christmas letters. Some missionaries were interned during the Second World War, and in her Christmas letter to missionaries in 1945 she writes: 'The safe return in these recent weeks of all our interned missionaries is a cause of deep gratitude ... They have much to tell us, but first they need some months of complete rest ... We are waiting impatiently for news of passages for the Commission which is to visit Ichang and Manchuria.' This was Isobel keeping in touch, informing and helping missionaries to pray for their colleagues and for the work of world mission.

Her platform addresses at this time showed her wide knowledge and care for the people concerned. She spoke with wit and poetical feeling, and her 'words' and her prayers made clear her belief and hope. In her speech to the General Assembly in May 1945 when, as WFM President, having reported on the past year, she looked forward to future needs of the mission field, particularly for more women to be sent, she said:

> Are we mere dreamers of dreams when we say that in the next few years we hope to find ninety-eight new women missionaries, nearly all with good professional qualifications as doctors nurses and teachers ... There are some characteristics of the best of the women of that younger generation of (possible) recruits which give us ground for hope – their adventurous and unconventional spirit, their interest in and knowledge of world affairs, their 'global' outlook, their sense of community, their eagerness to have a share in social service or the work of reconstruction, and when they are Christians, the possession of a faith which has already had to defend itself against attack, which is in some measure militant, objective and catholic.

What I find impressive is her vision, faith and commitment at a time when the Church of Scotland had no place for women in the eldership or ordained ministry. Providentially, people like Isobel Forrester could exercise their gifts of leadership in the sphere of foreign missions and in the ecumenical movement.

During her childhood and early married life, Isobel had experienced in her own family the pain of the disunity of the churches. After the Union between the Free Church and the United Presbyterian Church in 1900 and the subsequent judgement of the House of Lords, her father was evicted from his kirk, his manse and, he felt, from his life's work. Together with her husband, W. R. Forrester, a young radical minister of the United Free Church, Isobel experienced some of the difficulties associated with union where there are deeply held differences of conviction. In her work with the Girls' Auxiliary and the Sunday Schools, she herself had been able to prepare for the union of 1929. Her work with the Foreign Mission Committee added urgency to her recognition of the need for continuing dialogue between the churches.

After the end of the Second World War, there was a real ferment in the churches in Scotland to discuss issues of common interest, issues of faith and order, life and work and the mission of the Church. Between 1946 and 1950, church people, both lay and ordained, met annually for ecumenical conferences at a centre in Dollar in central Scotland. These conferences came to be known as the Dollarbeg Conferences. They were seminal for the Church in Scotland and provided a window on the world church. They took on a prophetic role in the subjects which they covered, and provided patterns for people from different denominations to study and worship.

As Mabel Small writes in *Growing Together*, her account of the ecumenical movement in Scotland from 1924 to 1964, 'The conferences provided creative inter-church fellowship, learning together through prayer, study and action God's will for unity of his people'. They produced a spiritually intelligent and active laity, giving an opportunity to lay people and particularly to women to take their place in the work of the world church. Themes for the Dollarbeg Conferences and the conferences which followed under the auspices of the newly formed Scottish Churches' Ecumenical Association set much of the agenda for the churches in Scotland for the second half of the twentieth century.

Isobel Forrester played a major part in the planning, preparation and leading of these conferences. She was stimulated and supported by her cousins, Donald and John Baillie, of the Divinity Faculties of St Andrews and Edinburgh respectively, and worked with some of her WFM colleagues such as Elizabeth Hewat, Allison Harvey, Naomi Oatts and Margaret Monteith.

Through these contacts and many others in the Student Christian Movement and the wider world church, they persuaded speakers of the stature of Lesslie Newbigin, J. H. Oldham and Hendrik Kraemer to come to Scotland. In preparation for the conferences, participants received study material such as Elizabeth Hewat's report on the role of women, and J. H. Oldham's pamphlet 'Work in Modern Society'. They were encouraged to meet in local study groups; and St Andrews' World Church Group is still remembered by many.

As an example of the ongoing work of which the churches were a part, the Dollarbeg conference on the Role of Women in the Life of the Church arose out of a questionnaire on this subject, circulated by the World Council of Churches – at the time still in the process of formation. The commissions which had worked on the questionnaire reported to the Dollarbeg Conference in 1947, and a report was prepared by Dr Elizabeth Hewat, on leave from India, and sent to Geneva. It is interesting to note that the Church of Scotland printed and distributed 3,000 copies of this 'Interim Report' for Scotland.

The second Dollarbeg Conference in 1948, recognising the tremendous political and social changes in post-war Britain, considered Christian witness in a changing world. Isobel Forrester presided, and the main speaker was Father John Groser of Stepney. Other speakers were Hugh Douglas, Helen McNicol and Nansie Anderson. The conference was attended by seventy-four people from eleven denominations or groups. 'They came', reports Isobel, 'because at the first conference they had felt such fellowship that they decided that they must meet again, and they left shaken and convicted and profoundly grateful for a new relationship with one another and a new commitment to a common task.' However, for the first time, the conference was made acutely conscious of the division of the churches, which necessitated holding two separate communion services when everything else had been done together. By the time of the 1949 conference, the Dollarbeg organisers were concerned to work on 'Expressing the Gospel in Action in Challenging Communism', with speakers like George MacLeod of the Iona Community and Donald Mackinnon of Aberdeen University. The next two Dollarbeg conferences dealt in depth with Work and Witness of the Laity and the Christian Doctrine of Work with Dr Hendrik Kraemer, Director of the Ecumenical Institute, and J. H. Oldham. The churches also tried to respond to changes abroad in the colonial structure of the world – people everywhere demanding status, dignity and significance. This was taken up at the first conference of the Scottish Churches' Ecumenical Association in 1951 with the theme 'Christians and the World Struggle'.

The Scottish Churches' Ecumenical Association (SCEA) arose out of the work of the Dollarbeg group and of the Scottish Churches' Ecumenical Committee, which consisted of official delegates of the churches. The constitution shows clearly the stage which the ecumenical movement had reached in Scotland. The Association was to be:

- a venue for discussion by churches of issues of common concern

- an organ for considering and effecting proposals by the World Council of Churches and the British Council of Churches

- a spearhead of ecumenical interest in Scotland, promoting knowledge and concern in individuals, congregations and groups.

Issues for the Scottish Churches' Ecumenical Committee were intercommunion, evangelism and peace. It should be noted that the 1952 Faith and Order conference had produced the 'Lund principle' that churches should do apart only what they could not do together. The Scottish churches were part of the British Council of Churches; and Isobel, as President of the SCEA, chaired the 1960 BCC Whitsun Conference at Swanwick. For many, she *was* the SCEA.

Before that conference, Isobel Forrester had been fully engaged in the preparation for the 1954 Evanston WCC Conference, and afterwards headed the post-Evanston campaign to Scotland. Geoff Shaw was temporarily employed to coordinate this work. Mary Levison remembers being sent all over Scotland to bring the experience of Evanston and of the worldwide church to people in their local congregations. In 1956, regional conferences were held to give people a taste of ecumenical experience. Out of this work arose the 'Tell Scotland' movement, in which the SCEA was fully involved and for which it prepared some of the study material.

By now, the agenda of the movement included concern for Inter-church Aid and Service to Refugees (later to become

Christian Aid). Isobel's own knowledge of individuals and their needs and her concern for our relationship with the developing countries led to her alerting people to the political changes planned for Central Africa. Her daughter Jean vividly remembers a conference in St Andrews about government plans for the establishment of a Central African Federation to which Africans in Northern Rhodesia and Nyasaland were opposed. Personally, this was my first introduction to Africa and to the part that church people could play in public affairs.

Links made by the Forresters with people like Orton and Vera Chirwa in Nyasaland later involved them in personal and political advocacy for people whom they had grown to know and love. After the Malawi cabinet crisis in 1964, these included Malawian nursing students in Edinburgh and Scottish missionaries, like the McAdams, who had fallen foul of the regime. They felt heard and supported by the Forresters. Our own family also experienced their ongoing care during the 1959 Nyasaland emergency and the years which followed. This was nothing new for the Forresters. Before the Second World War, they had been instrumental in getting the parents of one of the theological students out of Nazi Germany and had them staying with them in their house.

One of the most important achievements of the SCEA was the establishment of Scottish Churches' House at Dunblane. From the 1950s, the Association recognised the need for a residential centre where members of the churches and others concerned with the church and public issues could meet together for consultation, discussion and prayer. Isobel Forrester, John and Donald Baillie, Allison Harvey, Archie Craig and Robert Mackie were very much to the fore in planning. Scottish Churches' House was opened in 1960 with Ian Fraser as its first Warden. Ian had persuaded Isobel to be the third missioner with George MacLeod and Mervyn Stockwood at the 'Challenge of

73

Faith' Mission to Edinburgh University in 1940, and they had appreciated each other's special gifts. His contribution and that of Scottish Churches' House to the ecumenical movement and the life of Scotland was immense and is described in his recent publication *Ecumenical Adventure – A Dunblane Initiative*.

On Isobel's husband's retirement in 1959, they moved to Edinburgh, where her ecumenical and pastoral work continued undiminished. Throughout her life, her concerns for the Church were its mission and unity, its engagement with the secular world at home and abroad and the liberation of women's gifts. Her contribution to the churches in Scotland included vision, organisational skills, training and pastoral care. By upbringing, education and gift, she had a command of poetic and effective language that was invaluable and all the more memorable for the quality of her voice.

In spite of being neither minister nor elder in the Church of Scotland, Isobel Forrester played a supremely important part in the leadership and development of missionary and ecumenical work of the churches in Scotland, and is featured in Christian Heritage, Scotland. She preached in the University Chapel in Aberdeen, very much a first for a lay woman, and spoke and led in prayer at countless ecumenical and missionary conferences and committees. She was well known in BCC and WCC circles, and to people in South Africa, Malawi, Kenya and India for her own work and visits to family and friends.

Isobel Forrester died in 1976. At her funeral service, Archie Craig described the 'impetus which her enthusiasm and wisdom in counsel gave to the ecumenical cause in its pioneering days in Scotland and right on with undiminished zeal and zest through the difficulties which it later encountered'. He reminded us of her 'lively curiosity and intellectual vigour ... always testing conventional acceptances and hardened prejudices by criteria drawn from the heart of the Gospel, in the belief that there is yet far more to come forth from the Word of God than has yet been apprehended by the Church'. He spoke of 'the patience of her affections and the kind of quality of loving that does not dry up' and of 'her courage born of Christian faith and hope'. There are some of us, still alive, who can testify to this.

Our family has memories of furloughs in Edinburgh visiting the Forresters in Newbattle Terrace, enjoying the security of their beautiful home and garden. At the same time, we were stimulated and cheered by conversation with both of them that was full of understanding and humour. They were with us in our joys and sorrows. Isobel herself knew times of depression and sadness, and so was able to be with others at such times. She would turn to the words of one of her favourite hymns:

> Deck thyself, my soul with gladness,
> Leave the gloomy haunts of sadness,
> Come into the daylight's splendour,
> There with joy thy praises render.

Her work was 'people' work. She saw their potential and not just what they had already achieved. Her husband's dry comment was: 'You know, all Isobel's geese are swans!' She used her gifts of charm, persuasion and the force of her intention to encourage people to do what was necessary. We all saw in Isobel what it meant to be focused and disciplined, to be warm and faithful. The fruits of her labours are found in people. Her children and so many others have learned from her ecumenical and missionary vision and enthusiasm and, above all, her caring for people.

JULIE R. BAXTER

LESSLIE NEWBIGIN

EDITOR'S PREAMBLE

Lesslie Newbigin was something of an icon to twentieth-century ecumenists. This arose partially from the fact that he, starting as an English Presbyterian, became a bishop in the Church of South India – an event which appealed particularly to those of us of a 'confound the systems' persuasion.

I got to know him personally at a WCC Bossey conference called to discuss his book *The Other Side of 1984*. Much as I admired him as an ecumenical pioneer, I found myself on this occasion diverging sharply from his attitude to the Enlightenment. He seemed to find in this the roots of most of the ills of modern society; I, on the other hand, regarded it as a 'fruit of the Spirit' and, as such, a judgement on the churches of its day, not least in Scotland, where witch-burning was still tolerated.

Reading Duncan Forrester's lucid and learned exposition of Newbigin's theology, I am the more regretful that he is not still with us to engage in the current debate on a new Scottish enlightenment. How a 'public theology' with such a 'strong ecclesiastical emphasis' would play in current theological debate is an intriguing question.

When in 1995 my portrait of Robert Mackie was about to be published, I was delighted, first that Lesslie Newbigin – who had been his close colleague and friend – approved of it, and second, because he was happy to write an introduction. More than this, he travelled up to Edinburgh to speak at the launch.

He had a particular gift for friendship. Visiting George MacLeod in his last days, Lesslie would enter the room with: 'It's Lesslie Newbigin, George', in case he had forgotten (as we do).

LESSLIE NEWBIGIN'S NINE LIVES

I knew and admired Lesslie Newbigin and his writings for many years before he came to be our bishop in Madras in 1965. For the next five years, I came to know him better, as a friend as well as a bishop. And I was constantly amazed at how this friendly, unassuming man managed to live so many complementary lives simultaneously, and to be distinguished in each. Like a cat, Newbigin seemed to live nine lives, and in each of them he was a master who made a distinctive and important contribution – as theologian, pastor, bishop, ecumenical leader, social critic, liturgist, teacher, exegete and preacher. Not inappropriately, he has been called the nearest thing the late twentieth century produced to a 'Father of the Church'. He had an extraordinary breadth of sympathy and vision, one of the sharpest intellects I have encountered, a brilliant lucidity in exposition, a love of the church and a passion for the church's unity. And all his thought and action was grounded in his practice of discipleship.

Newbigin operated fluently in half a dozen languages. Hindu Tamilians loved to listen to his musical, classical Tamil; in Geneva he preached regularly in French, on one occasion puzzling his congregation because he enjoined them lovingly to strengthen *le foie* (the liver) rather than *la foi* (the faith)! And in English he was one of the most graceful and lucid theological writers of his generation. The corpus of his writings is huge by any standards, particularly amazing in the light of his constant and demanding pastoral and administrative roles. And his writing was characterised by a remarkable freshness. Not only did he rarely recycle his arguments again and again, but he engaged in depth with the debates and intellectual fashions of the day, whether that be the *Honest to God* controversy of the 1960s, *The Myth of God Incarnate* debate, John Hick's syncretistic account of the relation of the great world faiths, or the argument about Thatcherism and the future of the welfare state in Britain.

In three areas in particular, I think Newbigin will be considered to have made a particularly lasting and significant contribution – ecclesiology, missiology and Christian apologetics. His classic study of the church, *The Household of God* (1953), rose directly out of his role as one of the founding fathers, and one of the first bishops, of the Church of South India. It was not a simple defence of the South India scheme, but a fundamental recon-sideration of the nature of the church to which he was forced by the controversies around the establishment of the CSI, and his experiences in a united church which understood itself not so much as a new beginning but a rediscovery of what it is to be a church. He was constantly involved in reflection and writing on the nature and calling of the church, never in an apparently timeless way, but rather offering ecclesiological reflections arising out of constant wrestling with the churches and the ecumenical movement in which he was such a significant leader.

The second connecting theme in his writing, at least from his early days in India as a district missionary, was missiology, reflecting on mission strategy and respon-sibilities in village India, in the vast conurbation of Madras, and in a secular Western world which had lost living touch with its Christian tradition and was in an advanced stage of syncretism. He believed in the essentially missionary nature of the church, and was deeply influenced from the beginning by the thought of Roland Allen on the 'spontaneous expansion of the church' and the need to avoid a close linkage between mission and imperialism by following a Pauline model of evangelism. Mission was grounded, according to Newbigin, in Trinitarian belief and the divine ordering of history. His *The Open Secret* (1978) summed up his thinking on mission. It was based on his teaching after retirement from India at the School of Mission at Selly Oak Colleges in Birmingham.

As a Christian apologist, Newbigin was notable for keeping abreast of the issues of the day through a vast amount of reading, shrewdly adopting dialogue partners such as Michael Polanyi, Karl Barth and M. M. Thomas, with whom he often argued but whom he even more frequently enlisted on his side while he did battle with the rapidly changing theological fashions of the 1950s, 1960s, 1970s and 1980s. His apologetic was in a stream of books such as *Honest Religion for Secular Man* (1966), *The Other Side of 1984* (1984), *Foolishness to the Greeks* (1986), *The Gospel in a Pluralist Society* (1989), *Truth to Tell: The Gospel as Public Truth* (1991) and in countless papers, sermons and conference addresses. And in Margaret Thatcher's Britain he attempted, without success, to launch a Barmen-style theological declaration against the heresy of Thatcherism. He drafted 'Some Necessary Affirmations' in 1988, of which one was:

> The Church is required to warn all people, particularly those who have power and wealth, that every one will be finally judged on the basis of their treatment of fellow human beings, particularly those who have no power. Whatever hostility this may arouse, the Church cannot remain silent on this matter.

In his 'retirement', he kept constantly abreast of what was happening in theology, in the churches and in the society, and until shortly before his death he was still stirring audiences of students and church people with his urgent calls to relevant discipleship.

Ecumenical statesman? Pastor? Evangelist? Scholar and doctor of the church? Saint? Prophet? Lesslie Newbigin has been all these in ample measure. But many will remember him gratefully above all else as a disciple who throughout his long life sought to be faithful to the truth as he found it in Jesus Christ.

LESSLIE NEWBIGIN
AS PUBLIC THEOLOGIAN

Lesslie Newbigin was deeply shaped by the ecumenical biblical theology which emerged out of the German Church Struggle and the embryonic ecumenical movement in the 1930s, and which became a dominant orthodoxy in the early post-war period among Protestants. Newbigin became a major practical exponent of this theology, which he never deserted in the theologically swinging 1960s or the more sceptical and secular 1970s, 1980s and 1990s.

This theology was perhaps most clearly represented by Karl Barth, and the Theological Declaration of Barmen of 1934, of which Barth was the chief author. Newbigin himself for many years found the thought of Emil Brunner more congenial than that of Barth, but later in life seems to have moved in a more Barthian direction, making particular use of the kind of confessional approach represented by the Theological Declaration of Barmen. The new dialectical theology arose out of the deep disillusion with liberal optimism engendered by the First World War, the Bolshevik Revolution in Russia, and the rise of Hitler in Germany. Against the Führerprinzip, it set the Lordship of Christ.

The German Church Struggle and the Second World War appeared far more clearly than the First World War to involve a fundamental conflict of good and evil, of competing faiths, conflicting ideologies and contrasting loyalties. It was also understood as a conflict between the true Church and the idolatry of the *Volk*. The victory of 1945 seemed to many to be a kind of vindication of this particular theology and of the Christian Church over a demonic movement which had been of apocalyptic proportions. It is not surprising that after 1945 the theology that had provided a rationale for resistance to Hitler went through a period of great confidence, and the churches in many places prospered and attracted the brightest and the best of the younger generation.

This was theology which was confessional. It taught that the heart of the matter was the confession in word and action of the truth that is to be found in Jesus Christ; and such confession inevitably brought the believer into conflict with alternative ideologies and claims to loyalty which were totalitarian or idolatrous. It was an ecclesial theology in the sense that it saw Christian faith as inseparable from the Church; only in the Church could be faith be lived and believers nurtured; and more: the Church represented an alternative community and way of being.

It was significant that Karl Barth changed the title of his massive project in the early 1930s from *Christian Dogmatics* to *Church Dogmatics* – without the Church there is no Christian theology, and the theologian's primary responsibility is to help the Church to be the Church and to monitor and encourage its proclamation. This theology, then, claimed to be public truth, capable of engaging successfully in the public arena in battles against the brutal ideologies and political systems which degraded humankind by their falsity. It assumed that any serious theology would be significant in the public arena. It did not follow the 1960s slogan of 'letting the world set the agenda'; indeed the opposite. Theology itself should control its business, but its agenda was decidedly not confined to a religious ghetto or the in-house converse of a timid sect of 'cognitive deviants'; it was public truth. Barth's theology, to take the most obvious example, was public theology because it was serious theology which actually transformed the terms of debate. As committed and probing theology, it was also publicly relevant and constructive.

This was a public theology in so far as it claimed to be true in a way which was inspectable in the academy; but it was also an ecclesial theology which constantly emphasised its grounding in the life and witness and proclamation of the Church. It recognised a strong version of biblical authority: Christian theology must speak to the world of today and to its problems from within 'the strange world of the Bible'. There was an implicit emphasis on the unity of the biblical witness, exemplified, for instance, in the series of little books published in preparation for the Evanston Assembly of the WCC as Ecumenical Biblical Studies, with titles such as *The Biblical Doctrine of Man in Society*, *The Biblical Doctrine of Work* and *The Biblical Doctrine of Justice and Law*. The definite article is significant: the Bible is assumed to teach one thing on every major subject, and the movement from Scripture to doctrine was sometimes treated in rather too simple a way. But a galaxy of theologians and church leaders such as D. T. Niles from Sri Lanka and M. M. Thomas from India espoused this theology, delighted in the Bible and brought Christian faith vividly to light in the imagery of Scripture.

From early on, Newbigin stood squarely in the theological school I have outlined above. During his years in India and in Geneva, his days as a district missionary and later a bishop, as a leader in the negotiation of the South India scheme for unity and as a global ecumenical leader, his major coordinating themes were mission and unity. But he was, as an alien, somewhat reticent at that time on political and economic matters. When he returned to Britain on his retirement, he threw himself into theological debate and quickly showed himself still to be a doughty warrior as he crossed swords with those who taught that the incarnation was no more than a myth, or suggested that all religions boil down to the same thing, or capitulated to the onslaughts of Thatcherism on the welfare state.

Mission, unity and ecclesiology were still major themes, but Newbigin felt able as he had not been in India to engage as a theologian in political controversy. He found Britain, and indeed the West in general, to be in urgent need of a 'genuinely missionary encounter' between the gospel and post-Enlightenment culture. The heavenly city of the Enlightenment philosophers, he claimed, has failed, and indeed it has become demonic, for 'the project of bringing heaven down to earth always results in bringing hell up from below' (*Foolishness to the Greeks: The Gospel and Western Culture*, London: SPCK, 1986, p. 117). No longer is it possible, let alone desirable to attempt to restore Christendom or to return to a pre-Constantinian and pre-Enlightenment innocence. He could affirm, in terms that could almost come from Stanley Hauerwas, that 'The most important contribution which the Church can make to a new social order is to be itself a new social order' (*Truth to Tell: The Gospel as Public Truth*, London: SPCK, 1991, p. 85). But it must also seek to unmask and confront the false economic, social and political ideologies of the age as well as the simplistic pragmatism which is so characteristic of the Anglo-Saxon mindset. In an age when the West was in an advanced stage of syncretism, theology and the Church had to resist relegation to the private and domestic domain, and steadfastly confess the Lordship of Christ over the whole of life. With Calvin, Knox and Luther and indeed the whole premodern tradition, Newbigin affirmed that it would be blasphemy to suggest that economic and political behaviour lay outside the jurisdiction of theology. The task, as he saw it, was essentially public confession which simultaneously denounced falsehood and oppression and announced the good news of the gospel.

In the depths of Mrs Thatcher's reign, he tried, without success, to instigate a Barmen-style anti-Thatcherite Theological Declaration. 'No society can cohere and no government can continue to govern indefinitely', he wrote, 'when the exploitation of the weak by the strong passes a certain point and the political order has lost its moral credibility. The contemporary attempts of the governments of Prime Minister Thatcher in Britain and of President Reagan in the United States can only destroy our societies' (*Foolishness to the Greeks*, pp. 121–2). Newbigin himself was on record again and again as a prophetic figure who was not afraid to speak his mind on public affairs. When he visited South Africa under apartheid, he told the Minister of Justice to his face that he was under judgement by God for the injustices and atrocities perpetrated in his name.

RIGHTS, NEEDS AND WANTS

Newbigin both engaged in debates about theory and also addressed a few fairly specific political questions. Christianity, for him, represented in both theory and practice a third way, distinct from the orientations of Right and Left, which both shared Enlightenment assumptions. Both speak in terms of individual rights: the Right asserts each individual's right to define and pursue a specific good without interference on the grounds of a higher common good; the Left asserts that every person has the right to have basic needs met by the community. Each of us, according to the Enlightenment world-view, has the right not only to pursue happiness and fulfil our needs, but to decide what is our good, and what our needs are, for ourselves.

This modern world-view provides no way of establishing as 'public truth' some understanding of human beings and the goal of human life which would allow us to affirm an objective ordering of human needs or the good for human beings. In short, 'if there is no publicly accepted truth about the ends for which human beings exist, but only a multitude of private opinions on the matter; then it follows, first that there is no way of adjudicating between needs and wants, and second that there is no way of logically grounding rights either in needs or in wants' ('The Welfare State: A Christian Perspective', *Theology* 87 (May 1985), p. 179). Both the socialist and the capitalist accounts of human nature, Newbigin concludes, are false and lead to seriously flawed policies which are ultimately destructive of true community and human flourishing.

THE WELFARE-STATE DEBATE

The advent of the British welfare state had been greeted with tremendous enthusiasm and has continued to enjoy massive popular support despite criticisms and acknowledged problems, not least from the Christian churches, which have tended to regard it as essentially Christian in its concern for the welfare of all (see my *Christianity and the Future of Welfare*, London: Epworth, 1985).

Many of the problems that the welfare state ran into in the 1960s and 1970s had to do with inflated expectations and the insatiability of some basic human needs. Some people accused the welfare state of trying to play God by attempting to make the human condition unproblematic; others saw it as taking over in secular guise central functions of the Christian Church. The demand for health care in particular seemed to have no limits, as lifespan lengthened and increasingly expensive and sophisticated forms of treatment were developed. Many people began to wonder whether the economy could stand the escalating costs of the welfare state. Furthermore, on the one hand there were increasing worries that existing patterns of welfare provision led to an enervating dependency on a 'nanny state' and the erosion of economically vital incentives, and on the other hand it was demonstrated by a variety of researchers that the middle classes bene-fited disproportionately from health care, education and housing in particular. A welfare state which was based on communitarian and egalitarian ideals was clearly not working as it should.

Criticisms of the welfare state came from both right and left. The extreme Left had all along seen the welfare state as a palliative which obstructed the possibility of radical change by obscuring the harmful effects of a market economy. The Right increasingly saw market provision of welfare which allowed more choice to the client as the desirable way forward, and sought to replace universal provision with the provision of a 'safety net' of 'targeted benefits' for the weakest and poorest. The moderate Left continued to see the welfare state as a tool of social engineering rather than a safety net, but sought more cost-effective, decentralised and participative ways of providing welfare.

A Christian view must be in tension with both Right and Left, Newbigin suggests, and it will provide a critique of the past and some clues as to the way forward, precisely because it is 'public truth'. In a superb passage, Newbigin sums up his argument: what theology has to offer is true – the Christian view of the nature and destiny of human beings, which

> is that for which the Church exists as sign and witness. It is entrusted to the Church, not as one among a variety of options for the private cultivation of the religious life, but as the publicly revealed truth for which Jesus Christ bore witness before Pontius Pilate, the rock of reality against which all other claims to truth have to be tested. It is that human beings are created in love and for love, created for fellowship with one another in a mutual love which is the free gift of God whose inner life is the perfect mutuality of love – Father, Son and Spirit; that happiness consists in participation in this love which is the being of God; and that participation in it is made possible and is offered

as a gift to sinful men and women by the justifying work of Christ and the sanctifying work of the Holy Spirit. In the light of this given reality, all projects for the pursuit of happiness as the separate right of each individual human being are exposed as folly, and all definitions whether of want or of need are to be tested in the light of this, the one thing needful – which is to be, along with one's brothers and sisters, on the way which does actually lead to the end for which all things were created and in which all human beings can find their blessedness ('The Welfare State', p. 179).

This is heady, helpful rhetoric, far more theologically sophisticated than Frank Field's similar assertion that the ills of the welfare state can be traced back to a false and naively optimistic view of human nature. Field also advocates a return to the kind of balanced Christian understanding of human nature which was represented by R. H. Tawney. But Field takes the step that Newbigin seems reluctant or unable to take. He asks in quite specific terms what a welfare state that rested on a Christian view of human nature would look like. Field's thought is concrete; Newbigin is reluctant, perhaps on grounds of competence, to enter into specifics. Newbigin is strong and challenging on generalities and principles, but has little to say about application. But, as R. H. Tawney said, 'to state a principle without its application is irresponsible and unintelligible' (*The Attack and Other Papers*, London, 1953, p. 178). We look in vain to Newbigin for any serious engagement with questions of application, save in the life of the Church.

CHRISTIAN JUSTICE

Newbigin is sensitively aware of the problem of justice in a morally fragmented society, which I explore in Chapter 2 of my *Christian Justice and Public Policy* (Cambridge

University Press, 1997). He is convinced that there is 'no possibility of achieving an agreed definition of justice within the conceptual framework of secular liberalism. It is bankrupt' ('Whose Justice?', *The Ecumenical Review* 44 (1992), 308–11 (310)). The huge problems for society that arise from this confusion and uncertainty are not Newbigin's primary concern. He is more interested in presenting and commending a Christian account of justice which is relevant to the healing of society's problems and capable of coping with deeply entrenched injustice. Like the rest of us, he hears today 'a long cry of anguish and distress. And who can be deaf to this cry?' ('Whose Justice?', p. 308). But for him the task is not to amplify or relay that cry, but rather to unmask the illusions and confusions about justice which are so hurtfully dominant in our society, and then to 'set forth the quite different conceptual framework which is offered by the Bible and the Christian tradition'. This is the 'proper work' of the Church.

Justice is the other face of love, and both terms are given distinctive content in the Christian tradition. The true context of justice is the holy, generous, justifying love of God. Other ways of understanding justice lead to disaster. Let Newbigin speak for himself:

> Justice means giving to each what is due, but it is of the essence of the fallenness of human nature that I overestimate what is due to me and underestimate what is due to others. Thus we fight one another for justice with all the fervour of a moral crusade, and it eludes us while we tear the fabric of society to shreds. But what is really due to each person is to be loved and honoured as made in God's image and for God's love, then the struggle for justice (which is always necessary among sinful human beings) is protected from that demonic power which always takes over when I identify justice for me with the justice of God. We struggle for more justice in a world where absolute justice cannot be, but we live by grace as

debtors to the charity of God; and the stigma has been borne by another ('Welfare State', pp. 181–2).

True justice is relational. Its source is in the being of the triune God, 'in the eternal giving and receiving of love which is the being of the Godhead'. God's justice reflects his covenant faithfulness, even to the unfaithful and ungodly, indeed particularly in the justification of the ungodly. Thus 'at the centre of the Christian understanding of justice there stands the cross, not a symbol but a historic deed in which the justice of God was manifested in his covenant faithfulness right through to the point where the just died for the unjust' ('Whose Justice?', p. 310).

This is fine theology. But, because it floats free of concrete earthing, it is perhaps not hard to understand why Newbigin's thought on justice has attracted so much less attention outside the confines of the Church than the speeches of David Jenkins, or the Reports such as *Faith in the City* or *Unemployment and the Future of Work* which speak of implementation and go into specifics. It has its limitations as *public* theology.

THE CHURCH AS EXEMPLAR OF PUBLIC TRUTH

For Newbigin, the role of the Church is central. Involvement in the public arena is a form of confession and of mission, of which the Church provides a necessary hermeneutic. 'The missionary action of the church', he writes, 'is the exegesis of the gospel' (*Truth to Tell*, p. 35). The Sri Lankan minister and theologian, D. T. Niles, illustrates this hermeneutic process dramatically and in simple terms:

It is a common experience in India or Ceylon, when an evangelistic team visits a village, that in the meeting that is organised the small Christian community in the village will be sitting in the middle while the Hindus and Muslims will be standing all around. And, in that situation, the evangelist is aware that whereas he is pointing to Christ, his listeners are looking at that small group sitting in front of them. The message will carry no conviction unless it is being proved in the lives of those who bear the Name that is being declared. This village situation is the world situation too, and for good or ill it is still the Christians of Western lands who are sitting in the middle (D. T. Niles, *Upon the Earth: The Mission of God and the Missionary Enterprise of the Churches*, Madras: Christian Literature Society, 1962, p. 197).

Newbigin develops the image further, emphasising that in a village in South India, 'the local community *is* the human community. Your neighbour who lives in the next-door house is also the man you meet at work, in your leisure, on holidays and on work days. And even though Christians may be a small minority, the church stands in the village as a visible invitation to the whole community.' In such villages, the Christians rarely have a church building; they worship in the open or under the shade of a tree, visible to all. Here '[o]ne administers the sacraments and preaches the word to a group of believers surrounded by a wider circle of those who do not yet believe, but for whom also Christ came. One speaks to all, and the words spoken to the Church are heard by those outside' (Lesslie Newbigin, *Honest Religion for Secular Man*, London: SCM Press, 1966, p. 108). The message of the gospel is public truth which cannot be separated from the actual, day-to-day life of the community of faith. The life and nature of that community is a hermeneutic of the gospel.

If it is true that others understand the faith in the light of what they know and have experienced of the Christian community, the Church, so also Christians may not separate their understanding of justice, rights, community, welfare and so on from the fellowship that is called Church. For the Church is called to embody and manifest the justice and the love of God, and in fulfilling this task it manifests the fullness of life and the salvation that is promised in Christ. This is its mission, its calling, not for its own sake but for the life of the world and the welfare of the broader community.

Stanley Hauerwas provides, as it were, an explication of Newbigin and Niles's model:

> The task of the church [is] to pioneer those institutions and practices that the wider society has not learned as forms of justice. (At times it is also possible that the church can learn from society more just ways of forming life.) The church, therefore, must act as a *paradigmatic community* in the hope of providing some indication of what the world can be but is not ... *The church does not have, but rather is a social ethic.* That is, she is a social ethic inasmuch as she functions as a *criteriological institution* – that is, an institution that has learned to embody the form of truth that is charity as revealed in the person and work of Christ (Stanley Hauerwas, *Truthfulness and Tragedy*, Notre Dame University Press, 1977, pp. 142–3. My italics.).

Newbigin writes:

> In thousands of congregations throughout the world, it becomes possible for the church as a local fellowship to be an agency of God's justice. In its liturgy it continually relives the mystery of God's action in justifying the ungodly. In its common life and the mutual care and discipline of its members it embodies (even if very imperfectly) the justice of God which both unmasks the sin and restores relation with the sinner. In its action in the society of which it is a part it will seek to be with Jesus among those who are pushed to the margins. But in all this it will point beyond itself and its own weakness and

ambivalence, to the One in whom God's justice has been made manifest in the strange victory of the cross ('Whose Justice?', p. 311).

It is concrete actions by the local Christian community which express a special balance between realism and hope, and which embody in specific contexts the justice of God. 'The most important contribution which the Church can make to a new social order', Newbigin writes, 'is to be itself a new social order' (*Truth to Tell*, p. 85).

In this strong ecclesiological emphasis, Newbigin lays down a foundation for public theology which is often rather neglected elsewhere. His public theology insists that Christians' contributions to public affairs must be theologically based and distinctive. Otherwise, it is well for us to hold our tongues. And the institutional Church must take seriously for its own inner life the message it addresses to the broader society, trusting that in some way the life and worship of the Church, in all its weakness and confusion, may manifest the attractive truthfulness of the message proclaimed.

DUNCAN B. FORRESTER

RONNIE GREGOR SMITH

EDITOR'S PREAMBLE

I first met Ronnie Gregor Smith in 1947 when he was Editor of the SCM Press and I had just joined the SCM staff. At an introductory meeting, newcomers were asked to outline their particular interests. As a recent product – (some, not I, would say 'victim') – of Oxford's modern philosophy school, A. J. Ayer and all that, my preoccupation was, as it remains, the possibility and nature of religious language. I had developed a concern with the character of the interior conversation we conduct with ourselves in this area – intending some time to write on the subject. (In the event, I allowed life with four children to distract me.) Afterwards, Ronnie came and discussed shared responses to some of the issues: he is quoted as saying 'the renewal of faith is a matter of finding the right vocabulary'.

These reflections spring from conversations between Davis McCaughey, close friend of Ronnie Gregor Smith, and Harry Wardlaw, one of Ronnie's research students from 1959 to 1962, reminiscing in Melbourne recently. Reading of Ronnie's declared debt to English literature, I am reminded that Davis also studied that discipline before he turned to theology. I myself, although no academic, was schooled in the metaphysical poets and in Wordsworth, Arnold and Eliot before embarking briefly on philosophy. I now wonder what Ronnie would have made of that great twentieth-century Christian poet R. S. Thomas.

Indeed, as long as Ronnie Gregor Smith was living, working and writing, I had high hopes for Scottish theology. Sadly, however, he died in his prime.

'Ronald Gregor Smith may well be the most important English-speaking theologian of this generation ...' This is the way A. D. Galloway begins the splendid essay he wrote in 1969 as an introduction to the posthumous publication of Ronald Gregor Smith's work *The Doctrine of God*. Galloway then goes on to speak of him as having had a quite remarkable gift of prophecy, which Galloway defines as a gift of seeing what is there for all to see, but more than that – who sees into it and through it.

Ronnie Gregor Smith's ability to recognise creative potentialities out of which the future might be expected to grow was demonstrated in the way he picked up a clue given to him by a reference one of his teachers at New College made to Martin Buber's little book *Ich und Du*. The story came both from John Baillie, the teacher in question, and from Ronnie. In the course of a lecture, John Baillie quoted a paragraph from the German text of *Ich und Du* and gave his own translation. He then added a comment: 'Someone would do us a great service if they translated this important work into English. It would influence both philosophy and our enterprise very deeply.' At the end of the class, in Baillie's words,

> a young student came up to me and said, 'I wonder sir if I could borrow that book you were quoting from'. About a fortnight later he brought back the book with some pages of translation. He gave it to me and said 'Would this do?' I didn't know this student even knew German, but here he came back with the beginnings of a translation. I took it away and read it and brought it back to him saying I wouldn't want to change a single word.

Thus was born an association that led to the publication in 1937 of an English translation of this very important and influential book. It also marked the beginnings of Ronnie's own relationship to a writer who remained important to him for the rest of his life.

Another writer who captured Ronnie's attention in these pre-war years was Søren Kierkegaard. Kierkegaard's importance was widely recognised among German thinkers in those years between the two world wars, but he was much less well known in the English-speaking world. Ronnie's interest in German thinkers inevitably led him into an engagement with Kierkegaard's life and thought, however, and it was at about this time that he went off to Denmark to learn Danish so that he might write a thesis about this important Danish writer. But, when he read some of the more biting things that Kierkegaard wrote in his journals about scholars in succeeding generations, who would investigate and analyse his writings and then go on to write their theses about his thought, Ronnie abandoned all idea of completing this project. As he himself told the story, it was Kierkegaard who told him that he should not write this thesis. Nonetheless, he continued to read and to think about this great Danish writer, who, together with Buber, became one of the major influences in the development of his own thought; and, through his life as a publisher and a teacher, he did much to encourage an English-speaking public to read Kierkegaard's writings.

Yet Gregor Smith's way into theology was not in the first place shaped by this kind of study of German or Danish thinkers. It was not philosophical studies, nor classical studies, nor the study of the tradition of Scottish moral philosophy that laid the foundations of Ronnie's work as a scholar. He himself used to say it was the influence and teaching of Herbert Grierson, who held the chair of English Literature in Edinburgh University during Ronnie's years as a student there. Grierson was powerfully influential in introducing the work of John Donne and the metaphysical poets of the seventeenth century into academic study, and it was he who shaped the direction of the young Gregor Smith's thinking. The influence of Grierson and the consequent study of literature, both English and more generally European, were not only to colour Ronnie's work for the rest of his life, they were to influence what was for him the task of theology – a wrestling with what is elusive and a quest for a language through which to understand and evoke it.

From these days in Grierson's class, Ronnie was to form a lifelong association with David Daiches, who went on to hold academic posts in Oxford, Cambridge, Chicago and Cornell before becoming professor of English at Sussex University. He published on a wide range of topics, among them biblical themes. His beautifully illustrated book on Moses (1975) combines archaeological with critical awareness of developments in Old Testament studies, both Jewish and Christian.

Gregor Smith's friendship with Daiches and the time they spent walking and talking together in the Western Highlands played a significant part in forming the character of his later theological engagement. That Daiches himself was a Jew – like Martin Buber – sets a precedent for a line of connection, both intellectual and personal, that went through Ronnie's entire life. Ronnie said once that the renewal of faith was a matter of finding the right vocabulary. This emphasis on vocabulary is but one indication of his association with the literary tradition which had developed through his friendship with Daiches.

When he spoke of finding the right vocabulary, he was not talking about finding something that was already there. He was setting himself, or finding himself, in on intermediary path between those for whom the task of theology was simply to restate what had always been there, demonstrating time-honoured truths in new language, and those who wanted to find a whole new language, a whole new way of understanding, and who were confident they could fundamentally reshape the truth and find new and coherent ways of speaking about it.

This is not to say that Ronnie was centrally concerned with the questions which analytical philosophers were asking about the logical coherence of what we say, or the nature of our truth-claims. He did not ignore such questions, but his way of coming at them was rather different from the way that was common among British philosophers of that time.

This did not mean that he was uninterested in what the philosophers were doing. As editor of the SCM Press, he established and developed an important *Library of Philosophy and Theology*, and this inevitably brought him into conversation with some of the philosophers who were discussing issues of religious belief in post-war Britain. Yet he did not always find this an easy climate to work in.

After he had moved to the University of Glasgow in 1956 as Primarius Professor of Divinity, he was actually invited to join in a public debate with the philosopher Anthony Flew, but he was not prepared to accept this invitation. To some, this may have seemed like a tacit admission that he had no answer to give to Flew's arguments, but the nature of his reluctance was not as simple as that. As he saw it, the whole character of the kind of arguments Flew and his colleagues were carrying on served to misrepresent the real issues. It was in fact the *character* of such debates, with their polemical emphasis on abstract logical analyses, that he found distasteful. Such debating had too much the character of an adversarial contest, each of the speakers seeking to prevail, rather than being a real encounter between two human beings engaged in a kind of loving struggle, in which all the participants were each seeking to gain a measure of personal enlightenment.

For Ronnie, the pathway to the right understanding of Christian faith was a good deal more difficult than the current philosophical debate seemed to recognise; the right language was more elusive. The pathway of reflecting on the issues and truths with which theology had always wrestled would have to be found through language in which new perspectives were found and in which new realities broke through. He found himself more at home in the world of the poets, with their way of discovering the truth and expressing it. In particular, the poetry of Eliot was important to him, with its sense that language works tentatively to arrive at a sense of reality. This is the kind of sensibility that sets for us the path we must follow.

This meant that Ronnie's language was often allusive rather than definite. And his way not only led him to forging language and imagery through which he sought to express himself, but also led him into patterns of personal friendship and intellectual association. He took particular pleasure in the associations opened up by living in University Square, in the University of Glasgow, and he expended personal and intellectual energy in following them up.

This meant that Ronnie's work was not confined, in any narrow sense, to Systematic Theology. Some of his most significant contributions to the British theological scene were the outcome of his own personal friendships and associations: associations with Buber and Bonhoeffer, Barth and Bultmann for example. His time as editor of the SCM Press gave him the opportunity to bring to the English-speaking world the thought of such important theological thinkers whose work might otherwise have been much less widely known.

Inasmuch as he was not a system-builder, he stood in the company of Christian thinkers like Pascal and Hamann, Kierkegaard and perhaps Bonhoeffer. Some of Ronnie's most illuminating remarks are contained in his introductions to the work of others, and in all his writing he displayed the quality of a man who must say something but must not say too much.

In his view, this was not just a matter of choosing one approach to working in the field of theology, from a wide group of possible approaches; it is a way which arises out of the very nature of faith itself, the *tentative* nature of faith. One might recall here that gloss in the margin of the Deutero-Isaiah, found in the context of passages of praise and affirmation: 'Truly thou art a God who hides himself, oh God of Israel, our Saviour'.

Ronnie recognised that the God of faith is not the God of a philosopher or a dogmatician – a God who does not so much hide himself as disclose himself in what is said about him and for him. The God of faith is one whom we always have to seek, in ways and through language which finds its way forward with difficulty and in fragments, moments of illumination and clarity. Seeking to talk about such a God, Ronnie's language was epigrammatic, allusive and imaginative. The way he spoke about, or reacted to, problems constantly went beyond what might have been expected.

At the time of his sudden and tragic death, he had been working on a series of lectures to be delivered at Princeton Theological Seminary, and the draft of these lectures, which he had already prepared, was edited for posthumous publication by his friend and colleague Alan Galloway under the title *The Doctrine of God*. This title, chosen by Gregor Smith himself, might seem surprising in view of the influence that Kierkegaard had on his work. Kierkegaard once wrote in his journal that 'If it is really God's view that Christianity is only a doctrine, a collection of doctrinal propositions, then the New Testament is a ridiculous book'. Ronnie, I'm sure, would have been in complete sympathy with that remark. Yet he chose as the title for his projected Warfield Lectures this phrase: The Doctrine of God. He himself justified this choice on the ground that choosing any other title might obscure the seriousness of his subject matter. It might conceal that context of tradition out of which his faith and hence his lectures had come. This context of tradition he regarded as a necessary condition of the true seriousness of his work.

This stress on the importance of the context of tradition might again seem to be at odds with Kierkegaard's thought. In the later stage of his life, Kierkegaard expresses a growing impatience with theologians who spend their time presenting us with the traditions and history of Apostolic Fathers and church councils. 'Christianity', he says, 'speaks of God's willingness to become involved with the human race, but the human race has changed this into history about how God in Christ has involved himself with the apostles or history about how God in Christ has involved himself with humanity'. This Kierkegaardian dismissal of 'history' may seem to be a direct challenge to the importance Gregor Smith gave to what he calls 'the model of man as historical'. When we listen to how Gregor Smith understands the historical, however, we find the contrast is not so sharp. Yet there is a difference of perspective between the two writers. The historical model which Ronnie expounds views history as that which happens *between* human beings. It is interpersonal. In this, we see the influence not of Kierkegaard but of Buber. Kierkegaard's insistence on the singularity of the divine human encounter tends to obscure this interpersonal character. It is Martin Buber who first brought Ronnie to recognise its importance.

The emphasis on these writers who had influenced Ronnie's thought should not be allowed to blind us to his own creative originality. He was certainly not a mere exponent of the ideas of those who had come before him. He was clearly much more than that. Taking up what he learned from these encounters with writers who preceded him, he developed their insights in his own way, as he reflected on what it might mean to live in faith in the modern world. His thoughts were always developing, always challenging and always arising from the deep seriousness of a personal conviction that was committed to the dialogue of questioning and himself being questioned.

DAVIS MCCAUGHEY AND HARRY WARDLAW

MAIDIE HART

EDITOR'S PREAMBLE

I first heard about Maidie (an elder at Cramond Kirk during the incumbency of Leonard Small) from my fiancé, then on student placement there, and later from Leonard's successor, Campbell Maclean – friend and Highland maverick. She was a remarkable pioneer, never less than the Edinburgh lady in dress and behaviour, totally unintimidated by the male hierarchies but equally unintimidating to young women, inside the church or out. In spite of her multifarious commitments, her house was always immaculate, but those of us who coped less well never felt under judgement.

As Convener of the Scottish Convention of Women, she had a remarkable rapport with the wide range of women involved – trades unionists, militant feminists, Woman's Guild members (she herself had been President of the Guild). With considerable skill, she mediated their joint concerns. Without trying, she succeeded in subverting a common preconception of how church women would be. She was courageous intellectually and physically, latterly choosing to deny treatment which would ameliorate but not cure her condition. In her memory, a fund was raised for a series of lectures; and in 2001, at New College, I was honoured to chair in her name the first female Bishop of Hanover speaking on the WCC Decade of the Churches against Violence against Women.

'Equality, Development, Peace', the threefold aim of the United Nations International Women's Year (1975) and of its subsequent Decade for Women (1975–85), was also a focus of the World Council of Churches Ecumenical Decade of Churches in Solidarity with Women launched in 1988. Equality, Development and Peace also run like a golden thread through Maidie Hart's life and work in church and society. They are, after all, Kingdom of God concerns: Justice, Fullness of Life, and Shalom. Maidie had a very clear vision of the Church as a true community of women and men, a Church marked by wholeness and inclusiveness, and worked tirelessly with imagination and grace to realise that vision.

Born at Bridge of Weir in 1916, Maidie received her education at St Columba's School, Kilmacolm, where she was head girl. At St Andrews University, she graduated with first-class honours in English, and there she met Bill, her husband-to-be, a scientist whose career was in naval research. With their daughters Constance and Jennifer, they made their home in Davidson's Mains, Edinburgh, and were members of Cramond Parish Church.

Maidie's first foray into public service was as Brown Owl in the local Brownie pack. Membership of the Cramond Woman's Guild branch led eventually to her involvement with the then Home Board of the Church of Scotland. From 1967 to 1970, she was its Vice-Convener and Convener of its Women's Council. During that time, she made a significant contribution to the new Playgroup Movement, and her care for and support of the Deaconesses was particularly valued.

As Convener of the Home Board Women's Council, Maidie automatically became a national office-bearer of the Woman's Guild. The quality of her work and leadership skills resulted in her appointment as National President of the Woman's Guild from 1972 to 1975. As National President, she travelled the length and breadth of Scotland meeting, charming, stimulating and challenging Guildswomen wherever she went; but she never lost contact with her own congregation, where she was ordained an elder and served on the Kirk Session. Her period of office as National President of the Guild coincided with a new wave of the Women's Movement, and so wider opportunities and new dimensions of service and witness opened up.

She represented the Guild on the Women's National Commission, the government's advisory body under the Cabinet Office. Her contribution was so highly valued that she was elected to its Executive and several of its working parties, including the United Kingdom Coordinating Group for International Women's Year. As the only Scot on this group, Maidie took responsibility for setting up a Scottish Steering Committee to initiate and coordinate action for International Women's Year in Scotland. She called together long-established traditional women's organisations and newly emerging younger, often more radical one-issue women's groups, as well as individual women, and she soon had them working together. It was quite something at a big International Women's Year exhibition to see the stall of the women of the Communist Party sandwiched between those of the Woman's Guild and the Mothers' Union!

Under the guidance of the Scottish Steering Committee, which Maidie chaired, a Projects Committee helped to form a network of local groups throughout Scotland, each group focusing on the priorities of its own locality. Women from all walks of life took part. Women in other parts of the world were not forgotten, as money was raised for a women's literacy project in India in cooperation with the YWCA, and for a water project in Lesotho through contacts with War on Want, Scotland.

To continue this cooperation among women's organi-sations, and in expectation of a Scottish Assembly (for Maidie was a keen devolutionist), and with the encouragement of the then Secretary of State for Scotland, Harry Ewing, Maidie was instrumental in founding the Scottish Convention of Women (SCOW), which she chaired for a number of years. SCOW provided a focus for issues of special concern to women, a forum for women to identify and express their views, and a framework for common action. One positive feature of SCOW was the close cooperation between Church women, Trades Union women and other secular women's organisations. This was largely due to Maidie's grace and wisdom.

SCOW made submissions requested by government departments, the Scottish Law Commission and other bodies who were becoming aware of the need for women's perspectives to be brought to bear on decisions affecting the daily lives of women and men. Open conferences were held in different areas of Scotland in cooperation with District and Regional Councils as well as the universities, the Equal Opportunities Commission and the European Union. From the beginning of the Scottish Constitutional Convention in 1989, a SCOW representative made a contribution to its work.

As Founder President of SCOW, Maidie was very involved in organising special conferences concerned with the United Nations Decade for Women (1976–85). The government-appointed United Kingdom representatives to the United Nations Commission on the Status of Women, Baroness Trumpington and Baroness Gardiner, attended these conferences to hear for themselves what Scottish women's priorities were. A Scottish Joint Action Group had been appointed by SCOW to take responsibility for the Decade in Scotland, and this group published a Scottish Plan of Action for Women, the first in the United Kingdom. Inspiration for this Scottish Plan of Action came of course from the United Nations and was prepared for the Third United Nations World Conference, held in Nairobi in

1985. The Plan was also presented to the Secretary of State for Scotland, the Women's National Commission, the Scottish Trades Union Congress and others, asking for their support in meeting the goals of the Decade. These were the elimination of discrimination against women in seventeen interrelated areas of life, ranging from childcare, ethnic minorities, violence, education, employment, health and media to world affairs and the churches. Maidie was one of three women invited by the Women's National Commission to visit the former USSR; and women from the USA, China, Australia, New Zealand, Iceland and Poland were received in Scotland. In 1992, SCOW decided to disband itself, not because its work was done and its aims all achieved, but because other organisations of which Maidie approved, for example Engender and Women's Forum Scotland, were there to ensure that women's voices were heard and that their perspectives received attention.

Maidie's worldwide contacts were greatly enhanced when, as a Church of Scotland delegate, she attended the Fifth Assembly of the World Council of Churches at Nairobi in 1975. She was already experienced in ecumenism, having served on the Scottish Christian Women's Consultative Committee, but Nairobi led to a deepening of her ecumenical commitment and a widening of her ecumenical horizons. The theme of the Nairobi Assembly was 'Jesus Christ Frees and Unites'; and, as a result of the findings of two of its sections, 'What Unity Requires' and 'Structures of Injustice and Struggles for Liberation', it was agreed by the WCC that Women's Issues should be a programme priority.

Maidie became a member of the Inter-Church Relations Committee of the Church of Scotland, and again travelled from the Borders to Orkney with the Nairobi Roadshow, sharing the WCC Assembly experience through music, slides and talk and encouraging ecumenism wherever she went. Mainly at her instigation, the General Assembly of the Church of Scotland set up a Special Committee anent the Role of Men and Women in Church and Society. Maidie was its Vice-Convener for three years (1977–80), during which it consulted with experts, organised conferences, did theological and sociological research, held discussions with Assembly committees, met with and consulted ordained women, prepared an audiovisual study guide, sent out questionnaires to congregations and presbyteries, and reported annually to the General Assembly. The difficulty of denting the Church of Scotland's complacency on gender issues caused Maidie much frustration, even though the final report to the General Assembly of 1980 pointed out that 'the whole work of the Committee has been shot through with a basic concern for the total *mission of the Church* in and to the world'.

In 1978, the WCC launched a Study Project on 'The Community of Women and Men in the Church'. It was a joint project of the Faith and Order Commission and the Sub-Unit on Women, making clear that 'its fundamental character was that of an ecclesiological study, an issue of inclusive community, more than of a "justice" or a "women's issue" *per se*'. More people around the world participated than in any previous WCC study – in local groups and in regional and specialised consultations. They focused on three main areas of church life: theology, participation and relationships, in the light of the changing roles of women and men and of women's new consciousness. Maidie encouraged the Special Committee to be involved with all the issues raised in the study. Her ecumenical involvement and opportunities expanded further when she was appointed a Vice-President of the British Council of Churches (1978–84) and a Vice-President of the Scottish Churches Council (1982–6).

The BCC responded to the WCC Project on 'The Community of Women and Men in the Church' by setting up a working party to explore questions of humanity and sexuality. Their findings were published by Collins as a Fount paperback entitled *God's Yes to Sexuality*. In endorsing the Humanity and Sexuality report, the BCC 'affirmed the hope that the urgency of the matter would be borne in mind'. Maidie kept the issue of the Community of Women and Men before the BCC, but urgency was hardly the mark of their subsequent response. For several years, the BCC had looked at the possibility of setting up a Women's Unit within its structures. At an earlier debate on this matter, the argument for integration, involving more women in the existing male-dominated structures, won over segregation, establishing a separate structure for women. Maidie raised this issue again when she became a Vice-President and persuaded the Executive to arrange a consultation to give women a chance to share their insights and experiences and the churches an opportunity to learn of and from all that was happening in the context of the community of women and men.

As was to happen again and again, the invitation to attend the consultation was not taken seriously by church leaders, who passed it on to their women's organisations. Maidie, however, never gave up, and expended much time and effort on meetings and discussions. Memos, reports and papers, with detailed proposals for a Woman's Desk, were meticulously prepared and circulated. The eventual setting-up in 1990 of a Woman's Desk in the newly established Council of Churches of Britain and Ireland (CCBI), now Churches Together in Britain and Ireland (CTBI), owed much to Maidie's years of preparatory work and advocacy. Maidie also contributed much to the Scottish consultations whose satisfactory outcome was the inclusion of NEWS (Network of Ecumenical Women in Scotland) in the core structure of ACTS (Action of Churches Together in Scotland) in 1990.

Meanwhile, a whole range of contacts was being established with women in Europe, and in 1978 Maidie attended the Brussels Conference of European Christian Women which led to the setting-up at Gwatt in 1982 of the Ecumenical Forum of European Christian Women (EFECW), of which Maidie was a founder member. She also attended a WCC conference in Venice in 1979 on Human Rights and Mission and brought back an awareness of the need to expose women to areas of discussion and concern usually either dominated or ignored by men, for example human rights, sexism, especially sex tourism, and domestic violence, so that, being informed on socio-political affairs, they could make a fuller contribution to church and society. 'As church women, we were left in no doubt that the churches ought to be playing a strong supportive role in the whole process of social liberation and the struggle against exploitation, oppression and injustice in all their widespread manifestations.'

Maidie admitted that in Venice what had been academic and theoretical for her, especially in respect of racism, had become real, personal and deeply human. 'These were my sisters, my friends, whom I had grown to love and respect. All I could do there and then was commit myself to do all in my power to combat racism, overt or covert, and try to bring others to the point of recognition I had so belatedly reached.' Her capacity to listen, learn and change was a constant feature of her life of faith. In outward appearance, she might have seemed 'a typical Edinburgh lady', but this did not inhibit her from getting alongside the miners' wives during the strike in the 1980s, taking part in the Women's Mid-Decade Action Day at Westminster or joining a peace protest at Faslane.

The worldwide findings of the Community of Women and Men Study were gathered up at a WCC Consultation at Sheffield in 1981. Maidie and two other representatives of the Church of Scotland attended. She chaired a British preparatory meeting before Sheffield and arranged a follow-up consultation a year later. For the churches in

Scotland, she also organised a Day Consultation at Scottish Churches' House, 'A Chance to Change', to consider the issues raised at Sheffield, not the least of which had been spelled out by Jürgen Moltmann:

> Patriarchy is a very ancient and widespread system of male domination. Christianity proved incapable of successfully opposing this system. Indeed, quite early on, Christianity was already taken over by men and made to serve patriarchy. This had a crippling effect on its liberating potential. The liberation of women and then of men from patriarchy goes hand in hand therefore with a rediscovery of the freedom of Jesus and of the energies of the Holy Spirit.

Maidie continued to make a contribution to the Community of Women and Men by co-chairing a group of that name that met under the auspices of the Church of Scotland Board of World Mission and Unity, the community of women and men being regarded as integral to both mission and unity. This group presented a very important report to the General Assembly in 1986. It remains a useful resource for anyone today wanting to change the patriarchal mindset of the Church of Scotland, dealing as it does with how gospel needs turn into gospel gifts. It describes the underlying problems of the bias towards the masculine in our understanding of the human, and of 'the Church's task of pioneering the unity of humankind being seriously impeded' if there is not complete equality and sharing between women and men within the life of the Church. The plea for the language of worship to include all worshippers was made to presbyteries. Maidie understood this as a missionary imperative, not a trivial matter, and took every opportunity she had of challenging exclusive language.

The UN Decade did not bring about the radical improvement in women's conditions that had been hoped for. The churches had more or less ignored it. Therefore the WCC launched an Ecumenical Decade of Churches in Solidarity with Women at Easter 1988. A small Core Group of informed ecumenical and enthusiastic women was formed in Scotland with the task of promoting the Ecumenical Decade and its aims of:

- empowering women to challenge oppressive structures in the global community, their country and their church;
- affirming the decisive contributions of women in churches and communities;
- giving visibility to women's perspectives in the struggle for justice, peace and the integrity of creation;
- enabling churches to free themselves from racism, sexism and classism, and from teachings and practices that discriminate against women;
- encouraging churches to take action in solidarity with women.

Maidie cooperated closely with this Core Group, especially in organising a three-day seminar at Scottish Churches' House on 'The Community of Women and Men in Relationships through Theological, Social and Biological Spectacles'. A more representative number of male church leaders attended than had ever done before.

Along with these high-powered conferences and seminars, Maidie also formed an ecumenical 'Women Sharing' group of all ages, ordained and lay, from many different parts of Scotland. They met regularly at Dunblane to worship, share their joys and sorrows, get healing for their wounds from the struggle, and plan strategies for action. This was a very informal group with a real sense of sisterhood. Maidie's gift of friendship and fun, and her warmth and understanding, contributed much to those who joined Women Sharing. Her friendships were of course worldwide, and with her husband Bill she generously shared the hospitality of their lovely home, latterly in Dirleton, and of their delightful garden.

After her death in 1997, some of her closest friends and colleagues set up a fund to commemorate Maidie. A garden seat was commissioned, and was designed and made by Tim Stead, the Borders sculptor and furniture-maker. It is appropriate that it sits by the chapel at Scottish Churches' House overlooking the garden. Friends of ACTS as well as members of Maidie's family were present at its dedication. A lecture has been held each year to keep Maidie's vision alive, a vision of a genuine community of women and men in church and society.

At Maidie's funeral, reference was made to one of her favourite quotations. 'We must prepare ourselves for living with change as the normal state of life, the portable Ark rather than the solid structure of Solomon's Temple.' How well she lived with change and helped to bring it about, because of her deep and unshakeable Christian faith expressed in her own words: 'We always find *hope* in Him whose first resurrection appearance was to women in the garden, and in the power of His creative and ever-renewing Spirit abroad and available in our world'. The message from Sheffield all these years ago was one that Maidie continued to convey with passionate commitment, and is as relevant for church and society today as ever:

> Brothers, can you not hear the 'sighs too deep for words' of women who suffer war, violence, poverty, exploitation and disparagement in a world so largely controlled by men?
>
> Sisters, can you not see how the lives of men have been trapped by the effects of their having power and a supposed superiority?
>
> We speak as those who have been seeking to listen anew to Scripture ... and as those who have heard a word of God for today about a vision for our human life – a renewed community of women and men.
>
> We speak with urgency.

ANNE HEPBURN

MARGARET AND IAN FRASER

EDITOR'S PREAMBLE

Offered a London SCM post in 1947, I queried the possibility of Scotland instead, having been brought up south of the Border as an expatriate Scot. The then Scottish Secretary of the SCM, Ian Fraser, would need to agree. He did, although I am sure he had his doubts about this odd stranger. In his run-down office in Bristo Street (now long gone), he introduced me to the student President of Edinburgh SCM, James Blackie. Ian and I have remained good friends and sparring partners ever since.

A typical example of what happens to friends of Ian was my participation in the World Council of Churches' 1980s conference on 'Theology by the People' in Mexico City – a somewhat chaotic event – but stimulating, particularly in retrospect. As I write, he is at work in the USA or Cuba – it is difficult to keep track. At 88, he does not believe in the existence of jet-lag. He continues to surprise and to write. I recently saw him at the launch of his book celebrating the 150th anniversary of the birth of R. B. Cunninghame Graham at the latter's ancestral home, Gartmore House, before a remarkable mix of church, political and media people, with Sir David Steel, first President of the reconvened Scottish Parliament, as keynote speaker.

I was always struck by the way that Margaret's gentle strength, gaiety and courage provided an admirable complement to Ian's more extrovert characteristics.

RISK-TAKERS FOR THE KINGDOM

Leaving home to go to university, Ian said to his mother: 'If you are praying me into the ministry, forget it. That's not for me.' Leaving home to go to university, Margaret said to her mother: 'Whoever I marry, it won't be a minister'. He saw her across the Edinburgh University Old Quad Reading Room and decided he had to get to know her. With characteristic directness of heart and will, he immediately effected an introduction, and so began a friendship that grew into love. It was not a smooth courtship of unalloyed joy. Ian loved first and wrestled in prayer through a miserable winter season to give Margaret up if his love was not God's will for her. When Margaret's love later answered Ian's, she wept that she could not marry him, for she was not a Christian. He was happy to marry such a lovely, Christian unbeliever, but she would not come to him less than an equal, nor would she undervalue the importance of faith. Greatly helped by Isobel Forrester, Margaret found a personal faith in God's love that shone through in the loveliness and graceful hospitality of her life and which never lacked the integrity with which she had earlier faced her want of faith. The love of Ian and Margaret Fraser for one another, a love prepared to sacrifice for the well-being of the beloved, the Kingdom of God faith they shared, and the commitment of love and faith they made in marriage, patterned the whole of their life and work together as in struggle and rejoicing, tears and laughter, they gave themselves in answer to their calling to enjoy each other and work for God's Kingdom.

Ian Masson Fraser was born in Forres on 15th December 1917, the second of the three children of Annie Masson and Alexander Bell Fraser. When Ian was four years old, his butcher father went blind. Three years later, he and his elder brother were putting in two early-morning hours of work in the shop before school. At the age of 13, Ian was put in charge of the smoking shed, smoking ham and fish. Another of the responsibilities required of him was reading to his father. There was also an unspoken requirement to conform to his blind father's need to have everything mapped out, both the places and the people around him. Perhaps this childhood experience contributed to Ian's later critique of the power that controls and his willingness to challenge established conventions and institutions and explore the unmapped territory of church life and theology. His experience in the butcher's shop, where he saw the gap between the respectable church-going folk and the folk loitering on the street corners, was an early influence. Doing his homework in the living-room where the fire was lit, his father listening to the radio and the rest of the family engaged in their activities, prepared Ian to do his later theological work where life is lived rather than in the quiet of a secluded study.

Academic excellence won Ian dux medals at Forres Academy and gained him a general MA at Edinburgh University followed by a BD with distinction in Systematic Theology. His New College professors expected a distinguished academic career that would bring him to a chair in their midst. Ian chose a different course. His involvement in the Student Christian Movement at university gave him a precious freedom to think things through personally. A conversion experience answered his mother's prayer for the ministry. From 1942 until 1944, under the auspices of the Home Board and the Iona Community, of which he was a member, and wanting to root theology in reality, Ian went to work as a labourer pastor in the labouring gangs of the Tullis Russell paper mill in Fife. This new step in ministry and mission took place two years before the French worker-priest movement began, and alerted the Home Board to the possibilities of industrial mission. In 1943, facing the accusation that he had trained for the ministry and a possible future as a theological teacher but had turned his back on both, Ian wrote: 'This is not a rejection of ministry but the search for authentic ministry. This is not a rejection of theology but a search for relevant theology. This is not a rejection of scholarship but its completion.' On 27th July 1943, Ian and Margaret were married.

Margaret Davidson Dow Stewart was born on 24th May 1920, the eldest of four children. Her father was a butcher's assistant, and the family lived in Thornhill, Dumfriesshire. Intelligent, gifted in her ability to relate to others, she was head girl of Dumfries Academy and a winner of the Hannafield Bursary. At Edinburgh University, she gained an ordinary MA in 1941 and then a Diploma in Education at Moray House which led to teaching. Despite Ian's high academic prospects, she was willing to begin married life on a labourer's wage, sharing in the hard, insecure life of this new, uncertain venture. It was a willing choice she made again and again as she and Ian went from one new, risky venture to the next. She accepted Ian's judgement regarding his work, sharing with him priorities and values, but it was she who always, at each new stage, had a clear idea of what was to be the next work they undertook.

In 1944, their daughter Anne was born, and Ian had an interim appointment to Hopemount Church in Arbroath. He was then appointed the Scottish Secretary of the SCM; and the Fraser family, growing with the addition of son, Keith, lived in Edinburgh for three years. Ian gave a leadership that was, to quote Steven Mackie, 'exhilarating and disconcerting, supporting and challenging at the same time ... sometimes hard to take but it left most of us with a great admiration for him'. Margaret coped gracefully with the restrictions of sharing one house with six other households who welcomed children provided they made no noise at night. Ian was ordained during this time in 1946.

In 1948, Ian and Margaret began twelve years of parish ministry in the Fife dockyard town of Rosyth. Ian worked to release the gifts and ministries of the people on the basis of work on the Bible at every level of congregational life. He also served on the Town Council of Dunfermline, for five years as Convener of 'Streets and Lighting'. In 1955, he was awarded his PhD on 'The Social and Religious Outlook of R. B. Cunninghame Graham', another extraordinarily creative and adventurous Scotsman with 'a passionate concern for ordinary people, justice, a socialism and nationalism which is international, and an impatience with institutions both political and ecclesiastical'. Throughout these years, Margaret was an integral part of Ian's life and ministry. They added Ian junior to the family and, in the words of a member of their congregation, 'lived for one another, and did lovely things together for others'. A home-maker of high standard, Margaret managed so elegantly and shared so much on very limited material resources. She was an excellent cook whose knitting and sewing needles were seldom idle. She also put her intelligence and organisational gifts at the service of the Woman's Guild of the Church of Scotland, in due course serving as a National Vice-President. In 1958, Margaret was diagnosed with severe breast cancer and received the heaviest dose of radiotherapy ever before given by the Western General Hospital in Edinburgh. It is a cause of incalculable thanksgiving that she went on to live fully and joyfully for twenty-nine more years.

It was while undergoing her treatment that Margaret said: 'That's for us!' in response to Robert Mackie's approach to Ian about the common base that seven of the Scottish Churches wanted to set up. There was a row of derelict eighteenth-century buildings available in Dunblane, a need for someone to head up the project but no money for such a person or for the building. They took the risk. From 1960 to 1969, Ian was the first Warden of Scottish Churches' House, physically toiling alongside the World Council of Churches' international youth campers to clear the site and helping discover and dig out the ancient cellar that became the chapel. As Warden and as General Secretary of the Scottish Churches' Council which was revived in 1964, he worked at ecumenical development in the fullest sense, relating the churches in mission and developing relationships throughout society. People of all 'airts and pairts' came to consultations at Dunblane: artists, trade unionists, apprentices and church leaders. The list is long, and the vast range of topics considered includes housing, young people, poverty, international relations, prayer, sex, media and the world of the arts. In 1962, a consultation on hymn-writing saw a beginning dear to Ian's heart. Over 100 musicians took part during the decade of gatherings at Dunblane that followed, and it is generally recognised that the contemporary hymn explosion was ignited by the Scottish Churches' House hymn-writing initiative – Ian himself contributing several fine hymns. Margaret taught for part of the time at the nearby Queen Victoria School, where the boys found it hard to believe a minister's wife could be so attractive. Her loving hospitality, gentle wisdom and warm, clear-sighted affirmation of others reached out to all who found their way to the House.

In 1969, the Frasers moved from Dunblane to Geneva. A committee member since 1961 of the World Council of Churches' Department on the Laity, Ian was appointed to the staff of the WCC as an Executive Secretary in the Unit on Education and Renewal, with responsibility for the 'Laity and Studies' project and Leisure-Tourism questions. Margaret developed a great commitment to guest workers and became the liaison person between the WCC and 'Femmes de Pasteurs' who greeted migrant workers off trains. Ian was given the further responsibility of coordinating one of the five major study programmes decided on at the WCC's Uppsala Assembly in 1968: 'Participation in Change'. Asking how he should fulfil his double remit, he was informed he should find that out for himself. He made the option for the poor no mere theory but the basis for the programme. Instead of the traditional starting point with Western-based theology and study material, Ian gathered material through visits to Third World countries. Eschewing the traditional hotel-based stay, he lived with the people, travelling as they did, requesting a corner of a shanty in which to sleep and depending on the hospitality of the poor, their guest and never their patron. He was quickly trusted with their life stories, and the 'Participation in Change' programme was developed through sharing stories rather than abstract thinking. These stories of change actually happening at the grass-roots, of faith and hope against the odds, a rich treasure for the rest of the world, formed Ian's report *The Fire Runs* to the Nairobi Assembly in 1975, and many of his later publications.

Two years before Ian reported to the 1975 Nairobi Assembly, and while continuing as consultant and co-ordinator of the WCC programme, he became Dean and Head of the Department of Mission at Selly Oak Colleges, Birmingham, England. This was yet another new venture in which Margaret and Ian worked as a team, she offering hospitality to his students who represented over sixty different nations. She was also active in Weoley Hill United Reformed Church, which made her an elder. She represented them at the Multi-faith Resource Unit, headed up 'Tools for Self-Reliance' for Selly Oak Council of Churches, and was active in the World Day of Prayer. Ian continued his close involvement with the church of the future which he saw emerging concretely in small Christian communities around the world, and pursued his concern that 'research, reflection and life should interpenetrate one another if the product is to be called in any sense theology'. This, he maintains, is hard to do behind desks and within walls.

In 1982, 'retirement' brought them to Gargunnock in central Scotland and to the voluntary post of research consultant to the Scottish Churches Council. In this capacity, Ian and Margaret fulfilled an assignment from the British Missionary Societies and Boards to visit basic Christian communities in the Third World and to revisit ones in Europe, East and West, bringing back insights for the renewal of the Church in Britain. This Shalom Project also involved setting up in Scottish Churches' House the world's only resource centre on basic Christian communities. Accompanying Ian on most of his journeys, Margaret was a full partner in the work, collating, editing and translating documents and material in seminars. By April 1987, they had completed the main visitation of basic Christian communities in the Philippines and on the continent of Europe and had encountered a representative number in the USA. It was at a seminar held at the WCC's study centre at Bossey in early May 1987 that Margaret became unwell. Sent from Bossey with songs of the Kingdom, with hugs, tears and 'a quite tangible outpouring of love', Margaret and Ian returned early to Scotland, where a recurrence of cancer was diagnosed. Two weeks later on 31st May 1987, Margaret died surrounded by family and love.

Since 1990, when the Scottish Churches Council's successor, Action of Churches Together in Scotland (ACTS), was established, Ian has continued as a voluntary research consultant. His contact with the WCC and Bossey and his service on commissions and committees such as the European Advisory Council of the Commission on Filipino Migrant Workers based in Brussels has been ongoing. He continues in critical solidarity as a member of the Iona Community, committed to its prayer that 'hidden things may be revealed to us, and new ways found to touch the hearts of all'. Having had works published regularly through six decades, Ian has already brought out several books in this new twenty-first century. His recent world travels have taken him to Europe, Cuba, Australia,

China, the USA and elsewhere. Now in his late-eighties, he remains true to his personal catechism and calling: 'Question: what is Ian for? God's answer: Ian is for starters.' As Jim O'Halloran, a long-standing basic communities associate, expresses it: 'Ian dwells in the present, but in such a way that he is living the church of the future, a church where there is unity in diversity'. He continues to be himself: wise, just, generous, a great human being and good company, a unique teacher earthed in life and experience who enables others. Though far travelled from his Forres home and the butcher's shop, Ian has never left behind the habits and accents of his Scottish working-class background. Listening to ordinary folk everywhere, learning their languages, he sees value in what they do, and has established an astonishing rapport with lay groups of neglected and oppressed people throughout the world. Passionately committed to Jesus Christ and his Kingdom, he is an apostle to the laity who is revered worldwide by many as a prophet. He is a loving father, grandfather and friend.

I first met Ian and Margaret Fraser when they and I moved into the village of Gargunnock in the spring of 1982 – they to begin 'retirement', and I my ordained ministry. Their unfailing support and encouragement through those early years was an invaluable gift of God's grace. Until her death, Margaret graced my life with the gentle generosity and heart-healing, space-giving warmth and hospitality of her friendship. Ian, through all the years I had the challenging privilege of being his minister and since, has prayed me through the days and years, fed me with God's word and the vegetables out of his garden, made me groan with his puns and jokes, and awed me with the courage and passion, the earthiness and critical intelligence, the humour and simplicity of lifestyle with which he does theology as an integral, everyday part of living the Christian life. I miss the meetings of the Iona Community's Central Family

Group to which Ian brings his latest appetising culinary concoction (explorers don't need recipes) and the rugged, poetic reality of his prayers.

When I think of Margaret and Ian, I think of the salvation space of God's Kingdom, Margaret offering a welcoming and affirming space with her loving, thoughtful attention, Ian offering a sometimes difficult and always challenging space as he points you beyond comfortable limits and boundaries of thought and experience. I think of the Celtic interweaving pattern with its distinct and inseparable threads: heaven and earth, work and worship, everyday life and prayer; and of Margaret and Ian: two in one, each a distinct person with particular gifts, so beautifully complementing, enjoying and enabling each other, priestly and prophetic together in service to church and world. Centred on their beloved family, children and grandchildren, they were open in loving hospitality to all who crossed their path. Rooted in the here-and-now of the community in which they lived, they were global in their concerns and thinking. They shared a life of consistent integrity and boundary-breaking variety, with so many risky new beginnings, yet each a further exploration of God's faithful love. In them, we see saints of God's Kingdom with their immense gifts and also their endearingly human fallibility. Margaret, the day before she died, said that she was conscious of being surrounded by love, love here and love there, beyond death. Ian is now on his own and yet still Margaret's husband, longing for the love that is there and still passionately engaged in loving here as he continues to make the connections through worship, travel, writing and publishing, and just being Ian. In thanksgiving for their friendship, I offer this all-too-brief, personal appreciation and memoir and am grateful to all who shared with me their thoughts and memories. I conclude with two poems by Ian: one for Margaret and one for himself.

I love, my dear,
You, combing out your hair,
Quick, light step in a wind-swayed frock
Quick needle shining in shirt or sock:
Washing, gay on a dancing line
Dance of your eyes as they meet mine

Wife, witch, lover,
My joy and crown
Eyes whose sympathy soothes so much,

Voice which, at the dusting, sings:
Delicate hands, whose craftsman touch
Twines love around the commonest things.

                                                    1947/8

I walk the earth's thin crust, and underneath
fire surges, pressing on my feet
eager to swallow whole
dreams, ventures, o this fragile self
of faith and fear compounded. Nothing done
has a sure outcome. Loser take all.
Feet descend towards the abyss
fire waits to devour.

This is the way to live! Life's enterprise,
strangled and raped by cosseting
flowers on surprise. Our God contrives
footholds where none are seen: and meets
tentative steps of faith with ground
conjured from nothing. So our way
is sure, only when robbed of evidence.

I walk, this day,
Like one who walked on waves …

From 'People Journeying': Scottish Churches' House

CATHERINE HEPBURN

JAMES CAMPBELL BLACKIE

Six years of army experience during the Second World War, including the 'liberation' of Belsen and acting as judge in a de-Nazification court in Schleswig Holstein, served only to confirm James's sense of vocation to the ministry. The Student Christian Movement, of which he became United Kingdom Student Chairman, established his ecumenism which was to set the context for his work as Edinburgh University Chaplain. Our year at Union Theological Seminary, New York, from 1951 to 1952 occurred during its 'golden age' of Niebuhr and Tillich and afforded me experience of inter-faith counselling at Columbia under Ursula Neibuhr.

Within the SCM James became convinced by the insights of – among others – Joe Oldham, John Baillie, Archie Craig and Robert Mackie on the relationship between church and society, the concept of the 'frontier' and an unbounded ecumenism – a church for the world. Specifically, he had an understanding of what was called in SCM circles 'the University concern': the working-out of these ideas in a university context. When we met, I was secretary to a network called 'the Dons' Advisory Group', later the Higher Education Group, which explored the reasons for the failure of the great continental liberal universities in the face of Nazism. From such thinking came books like Sir Walter Moberly's *Crisis in the University* and the new movement to appoint university chaplains. Another aspect was an enquiry into the frequently unacknowledged presuppositions underlying the different academic disciplines. When initially approached over the Edinburgh University Chaplaincy, James refused, being happy to be – and to remain – in the parish ministry; but this interest in the relationship between Christianity and the university led him to yield to the persuasions of John Baillie and Willie Tindal.

Humour fed and flavoured his approach to life. Perfectly aware of a certain disdain for his department from the more abstract theological reaches, he maintained that nothing would persuade him to leave a faculty meeting for even five minutes in case his department should be abolished in his absence. (Naturally, from my particular standpoint, it was dogmatic rather than practical theology which might arguably lack intellectual credibility.)

Instituting full-time chaplaincies at the Royal, the Royal Edinburgh and Western General Hospitals in co-operation with the Medical Faculty, he associated the appointees with his departmental team for the training of all ministerial candidates, remarking: 'Perhaps we can ensure that at least they are not a *nuisance* within hospitals'. Bill Shaw, friend and colleague, said not long after his sudden and unexpected death at the age of 55: 'New College isn't as amusing now'.

Born in 1921 and brought up in Edinburgh, James Blackie was undoubtedly an Edinburgh man. He was, however, also a university man and a churchman. No doubt he made an impact when, after leaving school, he joined the Army, finishing up as captain in the Royal Horse Artillery. No doubt he made his mark as a student in the Faculties of Arts and Divinity in the University of Edinburgh. No doubt he proved a very effective, creative and popular minister in the parish of Carnock in Fife. It was, however, when he was appointed chaplain to the university that his major contribution began.

The university chaplaincy had been instituted after the Second World War, and the first chaplain was the Reverend David Read. He was a distinguished minister who later occupied the prestigious pulpit of Riverside Presbyterian Church in New York City. His was a hard act to follow. But Jim had his own gifts and his own agenda. He saw himself as pastor not only to students but to the whole staff – academic, clerical and general – the whole university community, in other words, and not only those with a commitment to or interest in the church. His extraordinary gift of friendship he extended to all, senior and junior, with the result that he gained the knowledge of and inspired confidence in a very wide spread of the university. This meant that he was able to make the new Chaplaincy Centre not only a place of Christian worship and meeting but also a centre of intellectual enquiry. Seminars of real quality on the ethical and theological questions of the day, led by heads of academic departments, were offered and were eagerly attended by many. In this period of chaplaincy, he practised and perfected the art of creating bridges – between students and staff; between conservative Christians and more liberal Christians; between church-goers and non-church-goers.

Here he developed his already lively interest in pastoral counselling, acting as first editor of the journal *Contact*. Here he established contact himself with the professors and lecturers in science, social science and medical departments who were later to prove so helpful. Here he demonstrated and helped others to see that Christian witness, service and care should not be confined to church or churchy circles but was only authentic when extended to a far wider circle.

The Chair of Christian Ethics and Practical Theology to which Blackie was called in 1966, was, as such things go, of comparatively recent origin. His two predecessors, Professor Daniel Lamont and Professor William Tindal, were distinguished scholars and ministers in their own very different ways. The holder's responsibility was, on the one hand, generally to offer instruction in the practical exercise of ministry, and on the other to teach and study Christian ethics. Under the former rubric, the students at New College, the great majority of whom were candidates for the ministry, were offered courses in pastoralia, preaching, Christian education, elocution and so on, all aimed at encouraging excellence in the practice of ministry. It was, however, an unfortunate fact that because the Practical Theology component, unlike the Christian Ethics component, was not an examinable subject for the BD degree, the not unnatural result was that it was not taken by most students with the seriousness and commitment normally given to academic subjects.

Into this Chair, Blackie was promoted after serving for two years as lecturer in the department. As Edinburgh's Principal, Sir Michael Swann, was later to write:

> Some people lean back in their Chair and take life easily. But James Blackie used it, as surely such a chair must be used, to extend his already extensive activities yet further, in teaching, lecturing, working parties, discussion groups and social service of every sort.

His Inaugural Lecture (1966) he entitled 'Method and Practice in Christian Ethics and Pastoral Theology', and here he gave a fair idea of what was to follow. He dealt with three areas – Christian Ethics, Pastoral Care and Theological Communication. He referred to the different stages of growth and pointed out that the study of Christian Ethics could only be conducted with sensitivity to the various interpretations evident in the history of the Church as well as to the questions of contemporary society. 'Are we as sensitive to the authority of God in His world as we are to his Word in the Bible?' he asked. 'If we are, we listen to the world and its dilemmas – we are not always preaching to it.'

In the study of pastoral care, he sought 'an education in attitude, flexibility and team-relationships, based on placements in real situations in which the role of the teacher/supervisor is vital and important. The student is helped to reflect constantly upon what he is doing, why he is doing it and how it is affecting himself as well as his clients as they both study this particular problem in depth.' He voiced his enthusiasm for the professional qualification in Pastoral Studies which had recently been introduced for the variety of specialist chaplaincies and for non-ordained pastoral workers. Here students would not only engage in theological disciplines but would also be offered courses supplied by other faculties in such subjects as Criminology, Human Relationships and Organisation of Industry and Commerce. (One amusing and unusual result of this procedure was of a student for the Diploma in Pastoral Studies gaining the class medal in Criminology!)

On theological communication, he saw clearly that real communication was only possible when the preacher understood the context in which he or she was preaching. In other words, it was necessary for the Church to take society seriously and to take advantage of the findings of sociology. The 'Church and Society' course which he outlined involved the students in active participation and observation in four different types of parish: country town, rural setting, city suburb, and church in an industrial setting. The students themselves would do the investigation and would report and reflect on what they had discovered.

As far as ministers were concerned, he took this opportunity of calling for regular periods of leave or sabbaticals for rest and refreshment – a call which was to be heard by the Churches, but only many years later. The closing remarks of his lecture are worth quoting:

> It seems to me that a function of a university department in this subject is not only to continue with the basic tasks of teaching and practical training, but also to make and create energy and time for the frontiers and borderlands of our subject – energy and time which is not always available in the parishes – but work done on behalf of the parishes.

What in effect happened was the conversion of Practical Theology into an academic discipline which found its place in the curriculum for the BD degree, with honours options being offered. This had a significance far beyond New College and indeed Scotland. At the University of St Andrews, James Whyte, Professor of Pastoral Theology since 1958, had been insisting that Practical Theology was not a collection of 'tips for ministers', but rather was to be understood as 'theological reflection on the practice of the Church'. Now, with the developments in the subject under James Blackie at Edinburgh, the subject of Practical Theology gradually cast aside its traditional secondary role and became more and more recognised in British universities as a legitimate academic subject.

Along with developments in the subject came developments in teaching methods. In 1975, *New College Bulletin* reported as follows:

> In the disciplines of P T additional methods have been devised to meet the needs for a balance between theory

and practice. *The project group* tackles a specific problem in Christian ethics and presents an end-of-term report, rather on the analogy of a working party. *Homiletics Seminars* bring four students together under a tutor to present and criticise seminars on set texts. *Role Play Groups* provide practice in pastoral counselling and experience of group dynamics. (The use of closed-circuit television in conjunction with role play allows the whole class to participate in the experience of the smaller group.) Finally, *Field Work* has become an indispensable adjunct to classroom learning. Visits of observation to church and state agencies and supervised pastoral experience in parishes, social agencies and hospitals provide both stimulus and challenge to the students' theological understanding. (The discipline of fieldwork supervision has itself become a subject of study by members of the staff, since it offers potential learning to all students of theology, whether or not they are ministerial candidates.)

While most of such methods are now familiar throughout the educational establishment, it is impossible to exaggerate the importance and novelty of their introduction in a Divinity Faculty in the 1960s and 1970s.

In Professor Tindal's time, the Department of Christian Ethics and Practical Theology was virtually a one-man department. Such assistance as he had, until Jim Blackie's appointment as Lecturer very late in the day, came from part-timers, usually ministers from local parishes. One of the reasons Jim was able to make such a dramatic transformation in the department was his ability not only to argue successfully for its enlargement but also to attract lecturers with specialist qualifications. All were theologians, but one had specialised in psychology of religion as well as in ethics, Alastair Campbell (see below), another in sociology, Robin Gill (currently Archbishop Ramsay Professor of Modern Theology, University of Kent at Canterbury), and one in Christian education, John Gray (see below). The result was that the department was able to provide research facilities and supervisory expertise in the broadest spectrum of subjects comprised in Practical Theology. It is no exaggeration to claim that, under him, the Department of Christian Ethics and Practical Theology was the leading resource and research centre in Great Britain, and as such gained a reputation in continental Europe as well as America.

Due to the expansion and quality of staff, an important aspect of the development of Practical Theology was the encouragement of research in the department. The new approach was found attractive by postgraduates, and a number of significant research projects were undertaken over a wide area. With the cooperation of outside agencies, notably the Church of Scotland, studies were completed which were to prove of considerable interest and service. One example was the rigorous (and confidential) enquiry into the mental health of ministers; another was a survey into church membership in the Burgh of Falkirk; yet another was a study of the effectiveness of Selection Schools for Candidates for the Ministry of the Church of Scotland.

Parallel with its recognition as an academic subject, Practical Theology under Jim Blackie became recognised as a legitimate professional subject providing qualification not only for parish ministers but for many others as well. Counselling, for example, has always been recognised as an important part of the minister's task, but it had traditionally been exercised on an intuitive, hit-or-miss basis depending on the minister's personality and sensitivity. The mid-twentieth century had seen a spectacular growth in professional counselling – 'the coming of the counsellors', in the language of an influential study (*The Faith of the Counsellors* by Paul Halmos). Appropriate theoretical and practical training of the growing band of counsellors required a professional approach. At New College, with the

Diploma and Certificate in Pastoral Studies, this was now provided not just for candidates for the ministry but for all the caring professions. This required close cooperation with other university departments, and it was part of Jim's genius that he gained this so easily.

Christian education was another area where a more professional approach was adopted. Traditionally in Scotland, since the time of the Reformation the parish minister had had the responsibility of supervising Christian education in schools. With the growth of the Sunday School movement throughout the churches, the parish minister had a duty to take an interest in Christian education in the congregation. As a rule, the minister had had little or no training for this task, as common sense and a knowledge of Scripture were expected to suffice. Now, however, there was a significant change. Dr John Gray, who had previously been head of the department of Religious Education at Moray House College of Education, was Senior Lecturer in the department, and with his enthusiastic cooperation and encouragement close liaison with Moray House made possible the institution of the Diploma in Christian Education. This was another professional qualification, not only for parish ministers but also for teachers of Religious Education in schools.

From what has been said so far, it must be obvious that, for James Blackie, Practical Theology was not an affair of interest only to the Churches. While it was essential to see it clearly and ceaselessly serving the Church in one way or another, it could not fulfil its remit as long as it did not recognise its responsibility for a wider sphere. Here it was by costly personal example as well as by academic and professional initiation that he so impressed his students, colleagues and friends. This is not the place to catalogue all the agencies and charitable activities to which he gave much time and effort. But it would not be inappropriate by way of illustration of the Practical Theologian's opportunity to mention four areas in which he made a particularly significant contribution.

The first was his personal contribution to pastoral studies by his founding editorship and continued membership of the editorial board of the journal *Contact*. The importance of this journal over the years has recently been recognised in *Spiritual Dimensions of Pastoral Care: Practical Theology in a Multidisciplinary Context*, edited by David Willows and John Swinton.

The second and quite different area to which his convictions led him and to which he devoted his energy was the Edinvar Housing Association. This was a surprisingly large association, requiring close cooperation with the local authority to provide housing for students and others, and Blackie was its first Chairman. Obviously, it was due to his enthusiasm and willing efforts that the Association thrived and succeeded.

The third area is one which perhaps above all testifies to the necessary concern of the Practical Theologian in general and in particular the regard in which Blackie was so widely held. He was Chairman of the Scottish Council for the Disabled, and it was to him that the Secretary of State turned to be Chairman of the Working Party on the Scottish Committee for the Welfare of the Disabled. Its Report in 1974 was well received and proved influential in the public attitude to voluntary agencies, now seen as an essential component of welfare, in addition to state agencies.

The fourth area, that of medical ethics, is arguably the one which the department has pioneered most successfully in the last forty years. Alastair Campbell – a member of the team – went on to set up a new department in Bio-Medical Ethics at Otago University in New Zealand before returning to the United Kingdom to the Chair of Ethics in Medicine at Bristol University. In Scotland in 2003, Kenneth Boyd, in his inaugural lecture to his personal Chair, spoke of Jim as his original mentor.

After Jim Blackie, Practical Theology could no longer be treated as the Cinderella subject of the divinity curriculum. Though his own contribution was tragically cut short while he was still in his prime, the developments which he and his team initiated by no means came to an end. His insights into the public nature of the subject and its professional potential have been shared and developed by his successors. It is crucial that this be recognised at a time like the present when theology may be in danger of retreating into the ghetto, cut off from public issues, language and life. Theology can no longer be seen as a matter of dogma and apologetics only: to be worthy of the name, it must be practical as well.

BILL SHAW

MARY LEVISON

EDITOR'S PREAMBLE

Mary and I met as students of the same subjects – philosophy, politics and economics (with an emphasis on the first) at the same Oxford college. We even shared a tutor – the radical Anglican scholar Dennis Nineham – for one term on Immanuel Kant.

We have never lost touch, and I have watched with admiration her patient and persistent response to her calling. I am, indeed, one of those to whom Robin Barbour refers as considering the General Assembly remiss in not calling her to be 'the first woman occupant of the Moderatorial Chair'. I am also one of those who, while comfortable within the reformed tradition, could wish that the Church of Scotland took more seriously the reformers' injunction *semper ecclesia reformanda*.

At last, however, in 2004–5 we have benefited from the first female Moderator, Alison Elliot, whose excellent credentials include being 'lay' and centrally involved with the Conference of European Churches.

Ever since the days of Cyrus the Great, many of the 'movers and shakers' of the Church have come from outside it. But Mary Levison, who can certainly be styled as one of the 'movers and shakers' of the Church in twentieth-century Scotland, is in every sense of the term an insider. She was born within the womb of the Church, she has worked all her life within its limits and structures, she has wrestled with it, and for all her life, and for all its faults, she has loved and served it. Mention of *Wrestling with the Church* is appropriate at the outset of this chapter. For that is the title of her autobiographical book (published by Arthur James in 1992) – and it is a book which tells her story, up to the date of its publication, with great honesty and clarity and charity and common sense. If the reader wants to know of Mary Levison, let him or her read that book, and then there would be no need to persevere with the reading of this chapter.

Mary Levison was born Mary Lusk in Oxford in 1923. Her parents, who were second cousins, were both committed Christian people, and both came from lowland families much influenced by the great Victorian movements of piety and renewal which characterised so much of Scottish life at that time. Her father, David Lusk, was a minister of the United Free Church and was appointed by it and by the Church of Scotland as Chaplain to the Presbyterian members of the University of Oxford.

This later developed into the charge of St Columba's. A scholarly and faithful pastor, David Lusk had shown his mettle by winning the Military Cross and bar while a chaplain in the First World War. Mary's mother, Dora Colville, was also a person of real spiritual gifts, who brought up her five children in the knowledge of the Lord and was herself interested in many aspects of the impact of the Christian faith on society. When Mary was 10, her father accepted a call to a congregation in Edinburgh, and the rest of her schooling was in Scotland. She then went to Oxford University, where she achieved a first-class honours degree in philosophy, politics and economics. So here was a young person of real ability, ready to venture forth into the post-war world. She had had some knocks already in the school of life: her mother had died when Mary was at St Leonards School in St Andrews, and two of her three brothers had been killed in the Second World War. Her eldest brother, John, survived the war and became a minister. He served faithfully for many years, most notably in Uphall in West Lothian – another firm block in the surrounding edifice of Mary's life within the Church. She had a younger sister, Janet, who worked for many years with distinction, especially in the realm of adoption, and who was tragically killed in a road accident some years ago.

It was natural that, after her mother's death, Mary as the elder daughter should choose to remain in Edinburgh if she could, to look after her father; natural too that she should immediately take on some form of service of the Church. She joined the Girls' Association of the Church of Scotland, and by 1948 had already become its Central President. This gave her a great opportunity to learn of ways in which and places where women could serve the Church. She found that, except for those who went overseas as missionaries, most of them did so not by entering the Church's full-time service, which in effect meant becoming a deaconess, but by going into one or other of the caring professions. Mary chose the road of becoming a deaconess. It is typical of her that she did this. Many people in those days would have said that someone as able and well qualified as she was ought to aim higher; but she knew what others profess to know but do not practise – that within the Church can be no higher form of service than to be a servant of the Lord, a deacon or deaconess in other words. Once set upon that road, she took the good advice given to her and went for the highest qualification she could achieve, a degree in Divinity at New College in the University of Edinburgh. There she was taught by some remarkable men – John Baillie, Tom Torrance, Norman Porteous, Oliver Rankin, James S. Stewart, William Manson and others – and emerged with a brilliant record, fully qualified to be either a minister or a deaconess (or, for that matter, a theological teacher, which indeed she did become when she later joined the staff of the Church's College at St Colm's, training men and women for missionary service overseas and women for work as deaconesses at home). But she could not be a minister of Word and Sacrament, not because there was anything in black and white in the law of the Church forbidding it, but because no woman had ever been ordained to that ministry and it was simply assumed that women were debarred from it.

So it was that in 1954 she was appointed to work as a deaconess in the parish of St Michael's, Inveresk, and there she worked as part of a team, doing everything that a woman could do and doing it, according to the testimony of her minister, very well. She was in fact setting up what would become a new congregation. In this process, she had to preach regularly, and the Church of Scotland had resolved that deaconesses with a full theological training should be licensed to preach. Mary saw that this was a strange procedure, for if the Ministry of Word and Sacrament is a single indivisible ministry, how can someone be 'licensed' to perform the first task and not also be ordained to perform the second? But she accepted it, no doubt believing that some day the two fragmented halves would come together – even for her, a woman – in a rounded whole. So, in 1957 she was licensed to preach, and later that year she was persuaded that she should go to St Colm's to be part of the teaching staff there. Then for three years from 1960 she worked as Assistant Chaplain – a new post – in the University of Edinburgh alongside James Blackie, who was Chaplain.

Thus her first ten years as a deaconess of the Church of Scotland contained a good deal of variety. But there had been more than we have told so far. Early on, Mary had been chosen to go to a number of international and ecumenical meetings, the most important of which was probably the Assembly of the World Council of Churches at Evanston, USA, in 1954, where she had been a youth delegate. She had also developed a number of contacts with the Deaconess movement in other countries, especially with the German Orders of Deaconesses to which she had been introduced while a postgraduate student in theology in Heidelberg and in Basel. That led into an aspect of her work which undoubtedly made her a 'mover and a shaker' of the Church. Perhaps the central question was 'what is a deaconess?' Is she simply a woman employed full-time or part-time by the Church, someone engaged in 'woman's work', or is she a member of an ancient and honourable order of 'servants', deacons and deaconesses, within the Church, finding their origins as far back as 'our sister Phoebe, deaconess of the church in Cenchreae' (Romans 16:1)? Until that and other similar questions were clarified, there could be no satisfactory planning about either deaconesses and their proper place in the Church or the relationship of the service of men and women in the one Body.

To cut a long story short, Mary Levison has played a central part in the discussions, the prayers and the plans as a result of which the Church of Scotland now has an order of presbyters, male and female, ministers of Word and Sacrament (also known as priests in large sectors of the universal Church), and also an order of deacons, male and female, servants of the Lord and of his whole Church. This is a great achievement, for it has brought the third order in the ancient threefold order of the Church's ministry back to the place which it seems that it originally held – an order in its own right, and not merely the stepping-stone to the presbyterate. The third element in the traditional form of the Church's ministry – the episcopate – is something to which Mary has yet to turn her hand.

Mention of the two orders of ministry, presbyteral and diaconal, brings us to the next stage in Mary's life and to the issue on which she is indeed to be honoured as a great 'mover and shaker' of the Church. Believing that she had indeed heard God's call to her to serve within his Church as a minister of Word and Sacrament, she presented herself at the bar of the Church of Scotland's General Assembly in May 1963, petitioning it to test her call to the ministry. It is worth stopping for a moment to notice the importance of the form of her petition. This is not in the first instance a matter of women's rights or of any feminist assertion or argument. It is a theological matter of her status as one baptised into Christ, where 'there is no such thing as ... male and female' (Gal. 3:28), and of a call, which the Church, rightly, has always claimed that it must test if the working of God's Spirit is to be truly discerned. There Mary stood, and there she stands in a real sense still.

Another element in this whole issue arises from consideration of the two orders, presbyteral and diaconal, mentioned above. It was argued in the 1960s by a number of people, the first of whom seems to have been Professor Tom Torrance, that men have a presbyteral ministry within the Church and women a diaconal one. This idea became a central part of the deliberations which went on within the Church of Scotland after Mary had presented her petition. To the idea that men have a presbyteral function and women a diaconal one, Mary applied her formidable analytic mind, and she showed beyond a peradventure that it will not do. She is said, therefore, with some plausibility to be the only person who has ever persuaded Professor Torrance to change his mind. This is in fact unfair, for he has changed his mind on other things.

Before we go further, one more thing needs to be said. It is best said in Mary's own words.

> I was ... frequently asked why I did not consider the ordained ministry of the Congregational Union of Scotland or the United Free Church of Scotland where ... my gifts and training would have been more fully used. I did not doubt for a moment that such gifts as I had would find ample scope as a parish deaconess, as indeed proved to be the case. But, more importantly, I knew myself to be inescapably held within the Church of Scotland. We do not choose the denomination to which we will belong to suit our own convenience. The Church is not a club in which one can transfer membership to the most congenial branch. The Church of Scotland was not only the Church of my parents and of my personal roots. It was for me the manifestation of the One Holy Catholic Church in Scotland, the Church both Catholic and Reformed ... That Church had chosen me, and not I it; so there was, in fact, no option for me but the Church of Scotland.'
> (*Wrestling with the Church*, p. 30)

She continues in her next paragraph:

> As to the capacity in which one might serve the Church, it has always been my conviction that the Church is unduly restrictive in its conceptions of ministry. People have an immense range of gifts to offer, and the Church's task requires people who can function in a multiplicity of ways. To restrict the professional ministry of the Church to those with an academic theological training, to expect them to be all of the same mould and all to be men would seem to be wasteful of many potential offers of useful service. I can't help asking, Why? I have the kind of mind – not particularly creative or imaginative but analytical which cannot refrain from asking questions about meaning and purpose. But obviously such questions are better asked from inside than from outside. So if the lines of ministry are to be redrawn; if, in particular, the distinction between

the ordained ministry and the rest is to be no longer made
on grounds of sex, then one has to plunge in wherever
the Church sees fit to put one and ask the questions from
inside. (pp. 30–1)

That was the base from which Mary Levison proceeded
in her petition to the General Assembly of 1963. Five years
later, after a tortuous history of motions and counter-
motions, debates, decisions and frustrations, that same
Assembly finally decided that 'women shall be eligible
for ordination to the Holy Ministry of Word and Sacraments on the same terms and conditions as are at present
applicable to men' (p. 106). The story is told in all its
complications in Mary's book, chapters 5 and 6, and cannot
be repeated in any detail here. But a few general points
can be made.

Of course it has to be emphasised that in all this Mary
was not alone. The Church throughout the world was
waking up to the fact that the relations between the sexes
and the position of women were topics on which elemental
changes of understanding and practice were taking place.
Some denominations preceded the Church of Scotland in
the ordination of women to the ministry, as has already
been noticed. The Church of Scotland's major southern
neighbour, the Church of England, and her local colleague,
the Scottish Episcopal Church, were debating, and indeed
sometimes agonising about, the position of women in the
Church. The very phrase 'the position of women in the
Church' was being seen now as a give-away: women are
the Church, or at least the larger part of it; and do we
talk about the position of men in the Church? Within the
Church of Scotland, attitudes were changing fast. Mary
had five female colleagues in the signing and sending of
an open letter to the members of the General Assembly
in 1967, the year before the final vote was taken. But it
remains true that to a remarkable degree the achievement

was hers. The form of her original petition, the speech with which she presented it to the Assembly, and her conduct throughout the whole proceeding impressed everyone who had anything to do with the issue as very remarkable. Composed (at least outwardly!), dignified, always logical and yet supremely persistent, here was a figure whom anyone could admire, and very many did.

Many different considerations and arguments entered the debate. The evidence about women's ministry in the New Testament and the early Church seems to have been less prominent than one might have expected, particularly when one is reminded that Christians of a conservative evangelical conviction have most often based their objections to the ministry of women on some fragments of evidence from the Pauline letters. Theological arguments, based on Scripture whether correctly or not, were used (see above), and there were also some strange theses about the proper understanding of the Genesis assertion of man made in the image of God. Plain prejudice also undoubtedly appeared. But the fact of the matter is that, so far as the Church of Scotland is concerned, the fight to recognise the ministry of women as valid in exactly the same sense as that of men was won comprehensively in those five years while Mary's petition was before the Church's supreme court, and it was she who won it. This is an achievement of very great significance, and for it the rest of us may all be profoundly thankful to God. It is also a significant tribute to her abilities and character that, since the vital decision to ordain women to the ministry was taken, there has been so little dissension on the matter within the Church of Scotland. In her own words:

> Ever since the winning of the argument in 1968, I have always held aloof from groups, committees and organizations promoting the right of women to greater equality of participation in the Church ... It has been

important to me that ... the whole debate should have
been as little adversarial as possible. That we have
achieved what we have without giving offence and
with a minimum of conflict is a matter for satisfaction.
Wrestling there has been, but that is surely a different
thing from fighting and campaigning. (*Wrestling with the
Church*, p. 109)

That was far from the end of Mary's life. For her life
changed when in 1965 she married Fred Levison and
became a minister's wife. For some, this might have been
the signal to embark on a new campaign, the campaign to
be ordained alongside her husband and take an immediate
share in his work on that basis. Not so with her. She was
content to take on the new duties in an age-old position;
and, although there were undoubted frustrations for her
when the local church in Berwickshire where they had
gone could not or would not give her scope for work nearby,
she was content to wait for her own ordination until they
had returned to Edinburgh and she was able to take up a
new appointment in the parish church of St Andrew and
St George, a chaplaincy to the institutions within that city-
centre parish – stores, offices and shops. At last she could
be and was ordained, fifteen long years after her famous
petition to the Assembly. Her husband was able to support
her in this, and his understanding has been a great help to
her. He himself came from a remarkable family of Jews from
Safad in Palestine, where his father, Leon Levison, was born
the son of a Rabbi, but was converted to Christianity by
his reading of the New Testament. Thereby another strand
was added to the rich fabric of her Church connections
and membership.

Mary has also done distinguished work in the last thirty
years in connection with the diaconate. She was President
of the Deaconess Council and convener of the Deaconess
Board within the Church of Scotland. She has not gone

without honour. The Queen made her one of her Chaplains in Scotland, and the University of Edinburgh awarded her the degree of Doctor of Divinity *honoris causa*. The General Assembly of the Church of Scotland has not seen fit to call her to be the first female occupant of its Moderatorial Chair, although there are very many who think that it ought to have done. It is some years since the death of her sister Janet left her as the only member of her family still alive. Now her dear husband has gone too, at a ripe old age. In his retirement, among other things, he wrote a lovely little book about heaven. So she is not alone, this humble, delightful, persistent and loving mover and shaker of the Church.

ROBIN BARBOUR

GEOFF SHAW

EDITOR'S PREAMBLE

My husband met Geoff through his student placement at Cramond Kirk, and they became and remained friends. Geoff's year at Union Theological Seminary, with its profound experience of the Harlem Protestant Parish, followed the year after ours, and later he baptised one of our sons.

It was difficult to see much of him if you were based in Edinburgh, because, for many years, he accepted the discipline never to spend a night away from the Gorbals; he would visit his mother and swiftly return. It was a very literal 'being there' for people. James was convinced that the Gorbals Group project was one of the most effective attempts at a new way of being the church in a city situation. His respect for the Group, however, made him determine that it should never be allowed to become a regular placement for divinity students and others who could unintentionally overwhelm it – always a danger for innovative situations in a small country.

The last time they met, when Geoff was Convener of the massive Strathclyde Region, James was delighted to have been kept waiting in an outer office, as it allowed him to charge Geoff – of all people! – with delusions of grandeur. They always ended up laughing.

Geoff Shaw, who died in 1978 at the untimely age of 52, is probably best remembered for his political activity. A Church of Scotland minister, he achieved the remarkable double of being elected as a Labour Councillor in the then largely Roman Catholic-dominated Glasgow Corporation, and subsequently being appointed the first Convener of the new Strathclyde Regional Council in 1975.

Geoff's impact on the political life of the West of Scotland was immense. Ron Ferguson, the author of the definitive biography of Geoff (*Geoff: The Life of Geoffrey M. Shaw*, Famedram Publishers, 1979), says that 'his political contribution, particularly in terms of mood, direction, agenda and style, was considerable'. There are many from that era who would still want to say that, had he lived, and had the devolution referendum gone the other way in 1979, Geoff could, and probably should, have been the first First Minister of the new devolved Parliament.

I met, and came to know and love Geoff, however, in both a narrower and a wider context. In 1961, I was a first-year Divinity student at Glasgow University, destined for the Church of Scotland ministry. My father, a Kirk elder in a respectable southside Glasgow church, was the one who introduced us. He had heard of the Gorbals Group Ministry, through Presbytery contacts, and thought I would be interested. So he found out when and where they met, and got me an invitation to go along. I was astonished, and excited, by what I found. Meeting in an upstairs flat in a close off a back lane in the Gorbals, I found three Church of Scotland ministers, two of them with wives and families, and a number of other folk – all living and working together within what was then still one of the worst housing areas in Europe.

None of the ministers, I soon discovered, was a 'proper' minister, preaching on Sundays and looking after a traditional Kirk congregation. Walter Fyfe was at that time a trade-union official; John Jardine was a teacher in a local secondary school; and Geoff was running youth clubs and football teams. But what really caught my imagination – so much so that, when we got married in 1963, my wife and I joined them, and stayed for the next eight years – was the radical approach of the whole Group, ministers, wives and others, to 'being the church' in that sort of an inner-city slum. To begin to understand how this came about, and the part Geoff played in it, we need to backtrack quite a bit.

Geoff came from a respectable and well-off Edinburgh family. His father had been an eminent surgeon who had died during the Second World War. Geoff had been educated at Edinburgh Academy and attended church at Cramond, where he came under the considerable influence of the noted preacher and eventual Moderator, the Reverend Doctor Leonard Small, and got involved in youth-club work. Initially intending to be a lawyer, his experiences in Cramond, and as a National Serviceman in the Navy, stirred a social conscience in him, and he decided to study for the ministry at Edinburgh.

At New College, the theologian who most influenced him was the Swiss, Karl Barth. Mediated through the radical teaching of Professor Tom Torrance, Geoff, as he always readily acknowledged, fell under Barth's influence in a number of life-changing ways. Through the writings of Barth, along with others such as Dietrich Bonhoeffer and Emil Brunner, Geoff imbibed an understanding of God's activity in the world that was both centred on the person of Jesus Christ and wholly committed to action in the human arena. This was to shape his whole approach both to ministry and to the life of the church in later years.

But what actually changed Geoff's life, in dramatic fashion, was the experience he had, along with Walter and Elizabeth Fyfe, of the East Harlem Protestant Parish in

New York. As Ron Ferguson puts it, 'It was in the crucible of East Harlem that Geoff Shaw became a twice-born man' (ibid., p. 39). For different reasons, both Walter, with his wife Elizabeth, and Geoff spent a year in New York in 1953–4. Two very different personalities – Walter much more radical both theologically and politically than Geoff – they came together under the influence of the families who made up a totally new attempt at 'being the church' in the teeming slums of East Harlem.

The principles on which the East Harlem Protestant Parish based its approach were simple and basic. Drawing on the experience of the French worker priests of the 1940s, and the Mission de Paris of Cardinal Suhard and the Abbé Michonneau, they saw the evangelising work of the church in such an unevangelised area as East Harlem as being, first and foremost, based on Christian presence. Before the gospel message could be heard, the gospel presence had to be experienced. And this could only be done, they concluded, by involvement at the deepest level with the lives of the people. The theological imperative of the Incarnation – God fully and totally committed to humanity in the man Jesus – was the bottom line. No parachuting commando of clergy and social workers could make an impact – only living there would do. So they moved in – lock, stock and barrel – and soon were immersed up to their eyes in the huge social and personal challenges of life on the East Harlem streets.

Space does not permit a fuller exploration of this radical experiment in twentieth-century Christian evangelism. Ron Ferguson treats it more fully in his book, as I do in mine (*Bridging the Gap: Has the Church Failed the Poor?*, Edinburgh: Saint Andrew Press, 1987), and a longer account has been attempted by Bruce Kenrick (*Come Out the Wilderness*, New York: Harper & Brothers, 1962). But when Geoff, Walter and Elizabeth returned to Scotland in 1954, and linked up again with John and Beryl Jardine in Glasgow, the seeds of a new approach to inner-city Christian evangelism had been well and truly planted.

They took a while to grow. Geoff found work for a spell in the flourishing Church House youth club in Bridgeton; Walter and Elizabeth worked for a while in Dalmarnock, while John, already a minister, retrained as a teacher. But when, finally, in 1958, with the cautious support of both Glasgow Presbytery and the Home Board of the Church of Scotland, they all moved in together into the upstairs flat in the Gorbals, what they were seeking to do was, in effect, establish an East Harlem model of the church in Scotland.

The principles behind the Gorbals Group Ministry were fourfold. First and foremost, to be there. Christian presence meant sharing as fully as possible in the lives of the people of the area. Sharing the same housing conditions, the same frustrations and negligence, the same dangers – but also the same solidarity, the same sense of community, the same laughter and tears. 'Gossiping the gospel' in the streets and closes and tenements, rather than preaching it from a pulpit in a church. For Geoff, this was expressed in his renting of a tiny two-room-and-kitchen flat in Cleland Street, where the car park for the renovated Citizens' Theatre now stands.

For nearly fifteen years, this flat was Geoff's home. Ron Ferguson has described Geoff at this time as 'a secular Gorbals monk', and 74 Cleland Street as 'his own cell' (p. 91). But, as Ron goes on to say – and this I can certainly vouch for from personal experience! – 'the only difference was that instead of being a place of quiet and contemplation, it was one of the busiest addresses in the West of Scotland' (p. 91).

From this 'cell', Geoff maintained a personal ministry to literally thousands. The door was always open. Through it, at all hours of the day and night, people poured. Boys in trouble. Parents in despair. Politicians, actors, journalists, colleagues, friends. From his 'cell', Geoff for many years administered the affairs of Scottish CND, not to mention the local Labour Party. The phone never seemed to stop – for a while, he even arranged an extension to our flat a few hundred yards away, so we could receive his calls when he was out. Even bath-time could be interrupted – his bath, a galvanised tub on the kitchen floor!

The danger here – the danger, in fact, with the whole principle of 'Christian presence' – is that we glamorise or romanticise it. It wasn't glamorous; it was bloody hard. And it wasn't romantic either. The Group always insisted that they did not see themselves as trying to be *the same* as their neighbours – trying to pretend that they were Gorbalonians. They always recognised that, while their neighbours were there of necessity (and many of them longed to get out), they themselves were there by choice, and could leave when they wanted to.

Danilo Dolci, the great Sicilian social reformer who visited the Group in the 1960's, spoke of his work as 'critical solidarity'. The Gorbals Group saw their presence there in a similar light. Thus, another of the principles on which they based their presence was that of a shared discipline. Drawing again from the experience of East Harlem, the Group undertook a discipline not only of presence but also of decision-making, of worship and of economics. Every Thursday, the Group met in one of their houses for a shared meal, for shared worship (including Communion) and for shared decision-making and accounting. Specific permission had to be sought, and given, to miss one of these weekly meetings. All their income was pooled, and each household lived at an agreed level, based on the then National Assistance amount. And every week, each household accounted for their expenditure, down to the last penny. In this way, the Group felt, not only were they seeking to make a witness to a certain gospel lifestyle, but also money was made available to undertake outgoing activity in the area.

This outgoing activity in the area was the third principle of the Group's presence in the Gorbals. From the start, they sought, in the jargon of the day, to 'let the world set the agenda'. In other words, the Group did not come into the Gorbals with preconceived ideas of what sort of shape their activity should take. Thus, very early on, three aspects of the life of the area cried out for their involvement. Young people, and families, needed support, especially in an area of chronic unemployment and huge social problems. Social conditions, especially the appalling housing conditions, demanded urgent and sustained attention. And, just as the East Harlem pioneers had realised that, if social conditions were to be changed, then political action had to be taken, so the Group found themselves very quickly deeply involved in the local political scene.

Geoff was active in all three areas. From the start, he ran youth clubs – drawing on his experience from Edinburgh and from Bridgeton. But these were not just clubs for local kids, to 'keep them off the streets'. If anything, the sort of youth work Geoff was doing was the precursor of what eventually came to be called 'detached' youth work. He used buildings, certainly – an upstairs warehouse, an old school. But he also worked on the streets, in the cafes, and in homes – his own, and other people's. His principle was clear: 'our role is to offer these young people a contact with an adult, which is both positive and voluntary' – in other words, they could reject him, but he sought never to reject them. After his death, going through his desk, we found a scrap of paper, a photocopy of which I have framed in my study to this day. It refers to a boy we both knew – wild, chaotic, but full of possibilities – and on it Geoff had written, presumably just for himself to see: 'Have known that he was very mixed up, and have proceeded on basis of refusal to reject no matter how foul'. And, if it doesn't sound too sentimental, I can recall a conversation between two local Gorbals mothers, talking about how

Geoff took their children on holidays every summer, and hearing one of them say to the other: 'All I know is, he loves these kids'.

As with young people, so with families and housing issues and politics: Geoff, with the Group and many, many voluntary helpers, really got, in Glasgow parlance, 'stuck in'. Nurseries, playgroups, an adventure playground, further-education courses (the Group talked about 'a university of the streets'), hordes of holidays (for children and families for whom a holiday was an unknown adventure) – the activities multiplied. Led mainly by Walter Fyfe, the Group sought to tackle the housing situation at its roots – exposing rack-renting landlords, attacking the negligence of the City authorities, arguing with planners about the so-called 'Phoenix from the ashes' which was to rise in place of the old tenements (if it had to be multi-storeys, then the Group argued, in vain, that these should be seen as 'streets turned on their end', with all the normal provisions of a street built in).

In later years, these activities of the Gorbals Group (even including the founding and publishing of the first local newspaper!) came to be seen as the precursor of 'community work'; and indeed when universities and colleges started offering courses in Community Work later in the 1960s, it was to the Gorbals Group that most of them initially sent their students on placement. At the time, though, the Group saw them simply as the inevitable result of 'letting the world set the agenda'. The issues were *there* – their neighbours were *there* – the Group was alongside them – let the work begin!

And what of the gospel and the Church? When the Group started, the established churches in Scotland were still seeing themselves as secure and 'successful'. The Iona Community, under George MacLeod and Ralph Morton (who strongly and consistently supported the Group), was pioneering new forms of church activity and worship, but mainly within a fairly traditional church context. The 'Tell Scotland' movement, inspired by the legendary Tom Allan and promoted by the American evangelist Billy Graham, had made a considerable impact on the life of local congregations. The Roman Catholic Church was still building huge sanctuaries to accommodate the thousands who attended Mass every week – and in the Gorbals, the major Christian denomination was the Catholic one, with the Protestants probably vying for second place with the growing Asian community.

But beneath these apparent success stories, the foundations were very shaky. To the majority of local Gorbalonians, whether cradle Catholic or cradle Protestant, the church 'was no' for the likes of us'. The Tent Hall, or school Mass, remained the residual worship memory for most of the Group's neighbours. And, from the beginning, the Group struggled, and at times fell out, over how a new form of church could grow in this rapidly disintegrating, secularised and depressed context.

Geoff's vision, to begin with, was very much on the East Harlem lines. He hoped to see small 'street front' churches appear on the Gorbals streets, and wrote at length about this, both for internal Group debates and for the Church authorities who watched the Group's activities with a nervous eye. Others in the Group were not so sure. For the majority of the members, the Thursday-evening meeting was all the 'church' they needed. For all of them, what they did, both collectively and on their own, was what mattered – and what bore witness to the faith that was in them. What Ron Ferguson wrote of Geoff could, I think, be applied to all the members of the Group, and to the Group as a whole:

> He tenaciously refused to separate speaking from doing, praying from acting, spirit from body, peace from politics ... He represents one alternative model of contemporary

Christian discipleship. He reminds us of long-forgotten radical strands in the Scottish Reformed tradition. He stands for imagination and risk-taking, over against ecclesiastical bagpipes, kailyard theology and 'survival without error', to borrow Iain Crichton Smith's evocative phrase from another context. (pp. 1ff.)

In the event, no recognisable indigenous church came into being as a result of the presence of the Gorbals Group; and the Scottish Divinity Halls, with one exception, never sent their students on placement to the Gorbals Group. The local mainstream churches decayed, just like their counterparts in all other similar areas of Scotland's urban jungles – and only now, over a quarter of a century later, are we seeing the shoots of some new and exciting church presence in the area. During the second half of his time in the Gorbals, my sense is that Geoff had moved away from expecting anything of this nature to happen. It was not that he had lost his faith, or his radical approach to Christian discipleship. Indeed, it was only during the latter part of his time in the Gorbals that Geoff came to see just how relevant Dietrich Bonhoeffer, and his Scottish interpreter Ronald Gregor Smith, was to the cause of the gospel in the late twentieth century in urban Scottish society. He was fond of quoting Bonhoeffer, from his *Letters and Papers from Prison*, with their incisive insights into 'religionless Christianity', or from his ground-breaking 'Cost of Discipleship', with its call to radical discipleship: 'When Christ calls a man, he bids him come and die'.

But, for Geoff, over the period, the feeling seems to have grown that if it was change that God wanted for His people in the Gorbals, then the way to bring it about was not through the Church but through politics. He kept closely in touch with the Group, although his attendance at the weekly meetings became increasingly sporadic as political duties and demands grew. A party activist from the beginning, he went on to seek election as a Councillor for Glasgow Corporation, eventually obtaining a seat as the Labour representative for Toryglen. When Alice Cullen, the sitting MP for the Constituency, retired, Geoff was persuaded to offer himself as a potential candidate for the seat. In the event, it was Frank McElhone who was selected – and, as they used to say back then, 'you didn't count the Labour votes, you just weighed them'! So Frank was duly elected the member for Glasgow Gorbals; and Geoff went on to undertake the immensely onerous and influential post of first Convener of Strathclyde Regional Council.

And it was at that point – May 1975 – that, in a strange and ironic twist, the Church, which up until then had, albeit somewhat anxiously, supported him financially, finally withdrew from him. The Group continued to support him – and his allowances as Convener were not insignificant – but we always thought it rather sad that, when one of its ministers had attained this incredibly influential position in the civic life of the country, the Church should have seen fit to appear to turn its back on him. But there it was.

And so he went on. He went on to work his socks off to establish a process and a procedure for the newly fledged Council that seemed to him to accord with all that he believed in and had sought to live in the Group. He listened – sometimes so long and so hard that his colleagues and staff were close to despair that anything would ever get done! As well as the Council, he chaired the Policy and Resources Committee, determined to ensure that the huge financial and resources potential of the new Council would be geared to meeting the widely differing needs of all its citizens. He worked punishingly long hours, often returning home to find boys sitting on his doorstep, desperate to talk far into the night. They were never, as far as I know, turned away.

In December 1975, Geoff and Sarah were married – in their living-room in his new home in Govanhill. Ron

Ferguson describes it as a 'marriage Gorbals-Group-style, with worship in the house and Gorbals friends and lots of children present'. I was immensely honoured to be invited to conduct the wedding – and we had a great day! And then life roared on – meetings, dinners, papers, negotiations, young people, travel. And the endless, endless grind of political life. He threw himself into it, heart and soul.

And three years later, he was dead. A heart-attack in March 1978, in his official car on the way to yet another meeting, led to the Royal Infirmary in Glasgow, a long period of hope and anxiety with Sarah and many, many friends, and a final collapse just over a month later. Ron Ferguson describes his death:

> Friday, April 28, 1978. John Harvey sat typing a stencil for the Sunday service, for St Mark's Church, Raploch, Stirling. The hymn was 'Lord of the Dance'. He was at the line 'I danced on a Friday, when the sky turned black'. The telephone rang. His friend Geoff Shaw was dead. He had collapsed while walking down the ward at 11.45 am. His heart had finally given out. He had at last let go. (p. 281).

I don't know how you sum up a man like Geoff Shaw. Of George MacLeod, ounder and first Leader of the Iona Community, Ron Ferguson, his biographer too, has written: 'He was a hero, not a saint'. In some ways, that could be said too of Geoff Shaw. He was my friend. I loved him – and I miss him still. I just hope he forgives me for writing all this about him – he hated this sort of thing!

For Scotland, and for Scotland's church, though, Geoff surely has much to say. About integrity. About vision. About commitment. About trusting people. About seeing where God is, and going to stand alongside him, no matter what the cost. About cutting the crap, and getting things done. About not wasting your energy on great blueprints and overarching plans for reorganisation, but rather starting where the need is and working up from there. Above all, of holding everything together in the bundle of life, and of giving it your best shot – all of it.

He died, we said, before his time. Yet, into his time he packed more than most of us could manage in twice as long. And week after week, at the Gorbals Group meeting, he shared with all the Group members in the reading from Luke's gospel, which they borrowed from East Harlem – the text that I think, above all, sustained him on his journey:

> The Spirit of the Lord is upon me,
>   Because he has anointed me
> To preach the Gospel to the poor.
>   He has sent me to heal the broken-hearted,
> To preach deliverance to the captives,
>   And recovering of sight to the blind,
> To set at liberty those that are oppressed,
>   And to proclaim a year when men may find
>   acceptance with the Lord.

JOHN HARVEY

EDITOR'S CONCLUSION

The origin of this book lies in a remark in a newspaper article, serving to remind us that one of the outstanding features of the twentieth century has been the dominance of the mass media. The communications explosion began with the burgeoning of the popular press at the start of that century – and later with film, radio and television, through to the Internet at its end. Propaganda by government of right or left, advertising on a global scale, the forces of religious fundamentalism – all have been given vast and unaccountable power through control of the media. Multiple sources of trivialisation and corruption surround us, and truth at any level is hard to come by. In Yeats's words:

> The best lack all conviction, while the worst
> Are full of passionate intensity.

From century to century, the Church continues to recover and discover. It seems to me of considerable significance that biblical truth derives its persistence and power from the fact that it is mediated by story, as in the parables, by image, by poetry and by action. Edwin Muir's indictment of Scottish religion as 'the Word made flesh made words again' has a special irony for such a Bible-centred tradition as ours. More than the Bible, however, theology suffers acutely from shifts of language and meaning and criteria of verification. One consequence of this is that the sermon, characterised mostly by assertion, has become an increasingly inappropriate mode of communication for the twenty-first century, lacking as it does any element of dialogue or general participation. This factor alone is quite largely responsible for the alienation of so many from the Church's life and message. A striking example of this has taken place in the area of biblical interpretation. In my teens, I found some understanding of historical context for both Bible and church a source of considerable enlightenment. Forty or so years later, bumping into David Jenkins, then Bishop of Durham, at the height of his notoriety, I said how astonished I was at the furore he had caused, as I had never heard him give an opinion which had not been common currency within SCM circles decades before. There has, I believe, been something of a 'trahison des clercs' in this respect, as their teaching ministry – where attempted – has borne few fruits.

But fruits there are. Many of the insights of our twentieth-century visionaries remain and continue to be reinterpreted. Several random examples within my own local setting, Edinburgh, come to mind.

One of the most alive and productive applications of Joe Oldham's 'frontier theology' is embodied in the Edinburgh Netherbow – an arts and storytelling centre – under its inspired director, Donald Smith. This is a fine example of 'a church without walls' in every sense of that phrase, and reaffirms the place of the imagination in the search for truth and its communication. Core-funded by the Church of Scotland, it has developed and adapted to changing circumstances over sixty years under a series of remarkable directors such as James Dey.

The Science, Religion and Technology Unit under its succession of distinguished directors, currently Donald Bruce, bears witness to a similar approach – the Church seeking to affirm the truly human along with others who share these values.

The Centre for Theology and Public Issues, based at New College under the Department of Christian Ethics and Practical Theology, continues to raise such issues in multifarious ways. Reading excerpts from the fascinating discussions among Oldham's Moot before and during the Second World War – including in its numbers John Baillie, Archie Craig, T. S. Eliot, A. D. Lindsay, Donald Mackinnon, Karl Mannheim, Walter Moberly and Michael Polanyi – is to be aware of the persistence of the same themes in church and society then and now.

'Oecumene' – the whole created earth: perhaps nothing reveals quite so clearly the churches' expanding horizons during the twentieth century than the recapturing of the original universality of this concept. From an initial geographical outreach accompanied by explorations of different church traditions, it is now perceived to demand a universality which is both extensive and intensive in nature. The ecumenism to which we are now called, 'that all may be one', leads us into unavoidable concerns for peace, justice and the environment, in solidarity with humanity as a whole. The 'why' questions arise in all societies; the 'scandal of particularity' has to be overcome and the circle of faith and no faith held in a tension of common concern.

'The Time Being', wrote W. H. Auden, 'is, in a sense, the most trying time of all.' The preoccupations of one's youth resurface in age – just possibly with more wisdom. Poetry is still at the heart of the communication of truth – the servant of the enlightened imagination; less perhaps Keats's affirmation than Wordsworth's:

> A presence that disturbs me with the joy
> Of elevated thoughts; a sense sublime
> Of something far more deeply interfused,
> Whose dwelling is the light of setting suns,
> And the round ocean and the living air,
> And the blue sky, and in the mind of man.

'A Time for Trumpets', however, is a time taken to acknowledge and celebrate our legacy. With equal urgency, the trumpets call us to assume our own responsibility for our own time.

NANSIE BLACKIE